THE OPEN DOOR

Arjang Mirzadegan

BALBOA.PRESS

A DIVISION OF HAY HOUSE

Balboa Press books may be ordered through booksellers or by contacting:

Balboa Press
A Division of Hay House
1663 Liberty Drive
Bloomington, IN 47403
www.balboapress.com
844-682-1282

Because of the dynamic nature of the Internet, any web addresses or links contained in this book may have changed since publication and may no longer be valid. The views expressed in this work are solely those of the author and do not necessarily reflect the views of the publisher, and the publisher hereby disclaims any responsibility for them.

The author of this book does not dispense medical advice or prescribe the use of any technique as a form of treatment for physical, emotional, or medical problems without the advice of a physician, either directly or indirectly. The intent of the author is only to offer information of a general nature to help you in your quest for emotional and spiritual well-being. In the event you use any of the information in this book for yourself, which is your constitutional right, the author and the publisher assume no responsibility for your actions.

Any people depicted in stock imagery provided by Getty Images are models, and such images are being used for illustrative purposes only. Certain stock imagery © Getty Images.

Print information available on the last page.

ISBN: 978-1-9822-7088-9 (sc)
ISBN: 978-1-9822-7086-5 (hc)
ISBN: 978-1-9822-7087-2 (e)

Library of Congress Control Number: 2021912740

Balboa Press rev. date: 06/22/2021

CONTENTS

ACKNOWLEDGMENTS

With so much thanks to my guides for the inspiration and all the people who helped: Lisa, Rich, Charles, Kay, Lina, and especially my son, Isaac, who did the heavy lifting and the majority of the editing to get the book to its final form. Thanks.

AUTHOR'S NOTE

Some of the names in this book have been altered to protect anonymity. In addition, this book is not intended to provide medical advice. The descriptions herein are based on my own experiences and insights, and I do not believe everyone has the same path.

Having once realized the presence of the Divine, one works up to the White Light! Once recognizing this non-dualistic state of consciousness, every being then works oneself down, finally arriving at the heart and thus seeing all the other people!

INTRODUCTION

THIS BOOK OF MEMOIRS AND ideas has been produced completely from my own life experiences and spiritual insights, by the *grace of the masters* from the higher dimensions.

My guides have asked me to write this book to share knowledge and to help reveal God's presence in every *self*, in every religious and spiritual organization, and in every atom of creation on this planet and throughout the universe. I have incorporated into these writings just enough of my experiences to impart a foundational understanding of my journey. Please join me on a journey through life's roller coaster of activities. I hope you enjoy my story and the tribulations within.

Everything in this book is true. I experienced it as it was written to the best degree my memory allows. These experiences continue to unfold within my life and within the lives of many others on this beloved planet. Believe what you will, judge if you must, but I write this book in order that all might accept the spark of their own *divinity*.

We are blessed, and we are the blessing of the light pouring forth from the universe's Great Central Sun onto the earth, now, through our bodies. As we learn to give love to all life and receive love from all life, we allow the light through us. We move toward this planet's time of mass *ascension* and spiritual acceleration. One need not leave one's body in order to ascend, achieving higher planes of awareness, or accessing the *light body* and dropping away the physical form.

As we learn to give love to all life and receive love from all life,
we allow the light through us.

I have traveled extensively and have found God everywhere, in every sect of temple and natural setting. It makes no difference whether you have been born Muslim, Hindu, Christian, Buddhist, or Atheist: God loves you. The *divine presence* is within you, as your most *authentic* self. *You are God's life*, and that is what all spiritual teachers hope to reveal. We have a choice as to how we use the energy of the *divine*. I would like you, the reader, to understand that I do not feel superior or inferior to anyone. We are equal, but we are all at different stages in our spiritual evolution. This body of work is meant for seekers of truth from any walk of life. I make no claims of sainthood, and I am not a monk. I still enjoy a good party and other physical pleasures. Also, I am not perfect in relationships, but I keep working on them!

What I have understood from my limited study of the Mayan calendar and culture is that we are experiencing a galactic sunrise. The more than 120,000 years of night have ended. In 1987, galactic dawn arrived, and on December 21, 2013, the sun fully rose on the galactic level. Furthermore, on the solar level, we are heading toward light.

It is my hope that in this new galactic daylight, people will see more clearly the corrupt governments, dictators, and various other control measures (e.g., energetic frequency control, monetary manipulation, television programming) that have remained hidden from public view. As people of Earth, as the new day dawns, we should not be able to hide anything dark within ourselves. This light should act on the level of the individual, the external, and the dimensional. As I see it, this light shift may require much work, and it will take time—especially on a governmental level.

Many souls I have spoken with are now experiencing multidimensional activity, or supernatural phenomena, such as *mass-minded activities* or feelings of mental togetherness. Many souls might be puzzled at this change in both the psychic and the physical world.

As the *light* comes in and the veils of this world are lifted, a view of other planes or realities may become more accessible. A new level of heightened awareness and integration with other beings of light and other dimensions may slowly be revealed. Now, integration of our *light bodies* can occur for everyone, coming from a new view of their selves as they release their old darkness, limitations, and negative perceptions.

It is my great hope that you will learn from these writings that everyone is truly okay and that we might understand how to simply flow with the universe. I understand that the less we resist and the more we trust all experiences, the gentler will be our process of collective consciousness and personal transformation toward peace and happiness.

The less we resist and the more we trust all experiences,
the gentler will be our process.

These changes, which I believe are now inevitable, have been in the works for a long time leading up to now. In the late 1800s, East met West when the first Hindu spiritualists went to the West to teach and share knowledge of yoga. Around the same time, European scientists went to the East to study ancient civilizations, and they returned with spiritual teachings. Unity churches were established in the late 1800s with a new take on Christianity, preaching the wholeness of humankind.

The planetary awakening became evident in the 1930s when the "I AM Presence" movement started. Beatniks expressed themselves freely in the 1950s, the Hippies flourished in the 1960s, and the idea of free love touched down on Earth. Even now, scientists theorize that the entire universe is made of light particles (i.e., electromagnetic energy), but it is still unknown what propels the light. On all levels of our consciousness and within all our world's cultures, humankind is experiencing a multidimensional awakening to our *divine reality of oneness*.

Everyone's natural state of awareness is one of enlightenment. Embrace the operation of God upon your mind; as you ask for it at some point, God will be revealed, and psychic and physical changes can occur. Embrace the truth that the *great light* loves us. This act is the process of letting go of all things we might have believed to be true: all fears and worry-based belief systems, as well as all negative opinions and judgments. Our fearful attitudes prevent us from realizing that we are already enlightened beings, cocreators with the *divine*. The darkness can no longer hide anywhere. People really are at one with the *source* and with each other. In *unity consciousness,* one person is no more privileged than another. We are one people. Therefore, it is time to work with each other for the good of the whole as we stand together *for* love and not *against* anything.

Everyone's natural state of awareness is enlightenment.

As we consciously open our hearts and trust more fully, we continue to merge into the greater transformational fields around and inside us, to receive our spiritual inheritance, and to have all our needs met. When we first feel thankful for life, we can continue to merge into the elemental kingdoms and into the angelic realms and into the greater beings and dimensions from all around the universe. Ultimately, we shall become one with ourselves and become perfect humans. So much divine light is now being poured out onto planet Earth, which is causing all darkness to be exposed: in our individual selves; our collective consciousness; and in the presiding principalities and powers, be they corrupt governments, monarchies, corporations, or priesthoods. The multidimensional veils continue to thin. There is a great division between fear and love as beings of light are being invited to merge with all aspects of divine life everywhere.

Consciousness is continually blessing you. The potential for Christ-consciousness is meant to exist within every one of us. Sathya Sai Baba, a Hindu holy man, said that only the earth provides the potential for beings to make an ascending shift, because the development of our brain stem on this planet is unparalleled in other realms or planets. Be thankful to have incarnated on this planet and for this unique potential. I offer you the blessings I have received from all the *ascended beings*—all deities, gurus, ancestors, and benevolent life forms in the realms and dimensions throughout the multiverses. May God's love fill you to overflowing, and thus may you realize and prosper in your *divine* inheritance. May God's love continuously flow to others through your heart-mind.

As only in the stillness all can be revealed, be still, holy child, and know, I AM.

MY STORY

MY NAME IS ARJANG SEYED Mirzadegan. I was born May 26, 1966, in Bonn, West Germany, to a German mother, Leni, and a Persian (Iranian) father, Madjid. My dad named my brother and me after Persian kings, or so he thought; my namesake was actually a prophet who drew his prophecies so that illiterate people could understand the word of God. My name was not common, even in Iran. My dad was born in Kermanshah, Iran. He moved to Bonn in the mid-1950s to study medicine.

My mother was born and raised in Bonn. She was a teenager in West Germany during World War II. She was born to simple farmers of wine and food. Her parents were loving people and earned their livelihood selling fruits and vegetables in the outdoor marketplace. They worked very hard every day, but I think farming was easy for them compared to the wartimes they had faced.

During World War II, much of Germany was leveled by bombs, and after the war, there was not much food or money available for most people. My mom suffered from the war and was a little nervous. For most of her life, she had anxiety attacks and didn't want to be alone. Though she had worked really hard for her father in the market, she had also studied well in school, and she was working as a secretary at the time she met my dad.

My father, on the other hand, was born to a noble family in Persia, stemming from a long line of lords, tracing his lineage back to Muhammad and all the way back to Abraham. My mother had a Roman Catholic upbringing, while my Persian father was raised in the Muslim faith. Because their cultural differences were too difficult to deal with, once they had married, they dropped their religiosity. When I was growing up, religion was almost never discussed around the house, and I do not remember ever entering a church or a mosque. Ironically, when it came to the divine, just about all I ever heard out of my parents was an occasional "Thank God." I only later in life found out they both had occasional private talks with God. My father took daily long walks while my mother spent most of her time in the house. Though both parents had some faith, each of them told me they did not really know what was real.

Through the Catholic side of my family, I experienced traditional Christmas celebrations, where at least the concept of the Christ Child, who bore gifts for humankind, was acknowledged. The only other Christian influence in my life occurred in first and second grade, via some nuns who came to our school on Fridays and forced us to pray, teaching us how to hold our hands. I remember it well because I was criticized for having the wrong thumb on top.

On the Persian side, my family members were all noble, highly educated, and wealthy. They were also unusually intuitive, with intense social awareness, and they believed in the concept of one

God. The family members who chose to emigrate from Iran, almost without exception, made their way to the United States and became even more educated and wealthy.

A very formal religious tradition ran through the Persian side of the family, at least until my father's generation. All the men's middle names were ancestral titles affirming the lineage all the way back to the Old Testament. Supposedly, only people who are descended from Muhammed have the title of "Seyed" in their name. All the men had this name until I chose to omit it from my son's name. I did this because my guru (doorway to God) suggested pride of family was a meanness of the heart, so I liberated him from that ancestral karma.

My dad told me the family had owned a third of Persia at one time, until the last shah's (king's) father, Reza Shah, reclaimed the land for the people. My Persian ancestors were land barons, and my father grew up in wealth and was highly educated. In fact, he received special permission from the shah of Iran to study medicine in Germany, where he met my mother. Though my father never finished his studies in medicine, he soon became an entrepreneur. In 1974, deciding there were better business opportunities in America, along with a chance to be closer to his younger brother, he sold his Persian carpet store, and the family moved to America. He invested in real estate, and I grew up living in different houses, apartments, and motels. My dad spent his time buying and selling real estate while my mom did the paperwork and cared for the household.

I felt my parents' love for me, but they misunderstood each other and frequently argued, with loud and intense, almost violent displays that scared me a lot. I think I was in shock much of the time.

Aside from that, they spent their time making money and partying with friends and relatives. They drank alcohol daily, which made their interactions even more difficult, as they were already under considerable strain from having to switch into a different culture. I think the second time Dad had to adapt to a new culture and language put a lot of pressure on him. I never fully understood when I was young, but when I was older, I realized Mom and Dad fought frequently. From the time I was eight, my home life was very intense. I would frequently hide in my room or behind the TV, trying to avoid their loudness and stay out of their way.

My parents spent the rest of their lives together, working on their resistances with each other and between their cultures. In their old age, they seemed to have more of an understanding of each other, and they were better able to work things out. It was like they had polished each other's diamonds.

I have a sister, Ingeborg, who is fifteen years older than me, and a brother, Bijan, who is nine years older. My sister stayed in Germany, as she had already wed. I never knew her well as a child, but we became friends as adults. The rest of the family moved to the United States in 1974—to Santa Barbara, California. I really liked Santa Barbara, with the stunning palm trees, the year-round mild weather, and the beautiful ocean. I remember playing in the water for hours and scraping the tar off my feet after swimming.

My brother left home the day he turned eighteen. He ran away to the US Air Force to "escape" my parents. He really could not wait to get away from them, especially my dad, as they did not see eye to eye. I remember witnessing many loud ego clashes.

Though my brother was only at home until my ninth year of life, he was instrumental in getting me into playing Frisbee—which is still one of my favorites—and he especially got me into martial arts. He began to teach me the basics at age five: punching, kicking, rolls, and so on. I continued a private and very casual study until age nineteen, occasionally sparring with others but without any formal training. I idolized my older brother. I didn't realize it until I was an adult, but he loved me unconditionally and vice versa. Even as a child, if I thought of him being hurt in some way, the thought alone was enough to make me cry. Of course, crying was not allowed. When I was a child, my parents would stop me from crying by discussion or by the threat of being beaten.

My brother and I enjoyed a kind of psychic communication. Our conversations were always easy, and we understood each other well. We have shared a psychic bond my whole life. I've always known when it was my brother calling on the phone. He not only taught me martial arts, but he also helped me believe in the supernatural, such as the ability to move material objects with my mind. I remember Bijan telling me about the old master in his martial arts class floating off the ground during the group's meditation practice. To this day, he and I need very few words to communicate an idea between each other, even though we took very different paths in life. He went more worldly and I more spiritual.

Perhaps because my soul was naturally joyful and simple, I remained largely oblivious to the continual personality clashes going on in the home. I spent much of my time playing alone; I climbed every tree in the neighborhood, made the best bows and arrows from natural materials, and spent hours playing my favorite fantasy game: cowboys and Indians. Sometimes I would pretend to be a cowboy, and sometimes, I would be an Indian. I spent hours alone, as my parents were not aware of my need for friends my own age. They focused their lives on doing business and succeeding in the new country. It seemed like they believed alcohol dispelled their stresses, but to me, they were often drunk and angry. I wasn't aware of the anger until one morning, when I was about seven years old. A coffee cup went flying across the kitchen and shattered against the wall. As the brown liquid slowly ran down, a long silence ensued, and an unconscious tension permeated my being.

After my brother moved out, I was left alone to mediate the life struggles and drunken brawls of my parents. My dad was often very jealous. My parents were always trying to make money, and their language barriers plagued them. I feel I was forced into an early maturation process. Frequently at a loss as to how to understand each other and create peace, they brought their debates to me. It was up to me to decide who was right and who was wrong. I believe this contributed greatly to my inability to focus at school and on my studies. Because of my parents' failure to communicate with each other and the stress of being in a new country, I was subjected to their daily raging arguments, which happened almost always after several drinks. I frequently felt as if I were the only adult present. One grace, though, is that their arguments were never directed at me. Also, they never really argued until the alcohol was involved. Even though Dad presented himself as stern, he was heartfelt and sensitive. Dad also had a telepathic link with me, but he used it for control rather than interaction. And my mother had love in her and was frequently intuitive, but she was also a little cold and not tremendously nurturing. My father's anger and need for control tensed the family dynamic. However, interestingly enough, it was this same anger—throwing a coffee cup against the wall and breaking it—that propelled me into a past-life regression: the moment I perceived as my fall from grace. It seems the same intensity reopened the crack between the visible and invisible worlds and my own timelines. Ironically, my memories of familial rage helped me make many profound shifts in my consciousness and shaped my personality traits as a young adult. We never know what will shape our reality and destinies.

In Santa Barbara, I began to learn English in the third grade. Until that point, I had mainly spoken German and Persian, my parents' native tongues. Being a first-generation transplant was scary. Even though I excelled in math, English was challenging. I developed a negative self-image, which stayed with me all the way through my school years. I was plagued by self-doubt, and I lacked focus. Even now, some days, I actually think it is ridiculous that I am writing this book. It is still difficult to deal with self-doubt, but I am facing myself now.

The English alphabet, fortunately, is the same as the German one. And because the spoken sounds were so similar, I learned to speak English quickly. I had to do a lot of translation work for my family. Frequently, the chore of answering the family phone fell to me. Although both parents were highly intelligent, it was difficult for them to master another language and culture so late in life, both already in their late forties. Dad and Mom did manage to become proficient, and they passed their citizenship tests, but they never excelled in English. Thus, I never received any help from them in school. In fact, I would give them an English spelling test every week to help them learn. Honestly, I never liked school, and without their involvement, I slacked heavily. I really did the minimum I could get away with.

I have no idea how my parents managed to excel at business (except by grace), but we were always financially stable. It remains a mystery to me because my parents were almost always drunk by the time I got home from school. Growing up, I did not realize how much their dysfunction toward each other affected my grades and my personal relationships. It is difficult to focus when one is concerned for others. Also, without an example of what a healthy relationship looks like, we tend to reach for dys-*function*.

I always had fun with my brother when he came home to visit. Although he was subject to my parents' dysfunction, I saw he had also incarnated with his own past life damage, which I recognized in him as I cleared my own past and present life damage as an adult. Although he is very conscious, I feel that because he has not completely cleared his own past-life trauma or current blocks with my parents and can sometimes act out of guilt or blame, he cannot yet clear himself of the lifetimes of emotional baggage. I believe he will eventually do his spiritual work and come to understand that we choose our own parents to clear our past karmic debts. This insight allowed me to do further work on myself. I spent many hours and years soul-searching for my own identity. The search for the true self included the reduction of my personality (ego), by killing every negative or unhelpful prior belief system I had developed. I expanded mentally and began to embrace my interactions with the world around me, with nature, and with others. This search improved my interactions with myself and others in spite of my own insecurities and others' human frailties and faults.

Because of my family's lack of awareness, I spent much time alone and often felt ignored. With a proper upbringing, I might have flourished more in the world as a worldly person, focused on fame or making money, which might have easily distracted me from my relationship with God. Because of this realization that I could have become anything, I perceive my parents as great gifts to me. They stimulated my own path of personal growth as many of their faults were perfect for my *soul* evolution.

My parents put me to work at a young age, around nine years old, for just a few hours a day. It began with gardening, weeding, watering, and mowing lawns. I helped Dad paint a little and then a lot more when I got older. We opened a secondhand store on State Street in Santa Barbara, and I was running the register by the age of nine. At this young age, I had every sales tax increment memorized, from one to one hundred dollars.

However, I felt like an outsider. I had no group of people—there was no clique for me to join. For me, spending a lot of time alone was normal. Even at home, my parents never played with me, and my brother was so much older. I spent most of my time watching television and swimming.

Water was the most healing environment for me. Being immersed in water was wonderful as long as someone else was around. But as soon as I was alone, I would become overwhelmed by an irrational fear of sharks.

Sharks were not my only fear. When the lights went out at night, I always went to bed afraid, and I tucked my blanket in on all sides so nothing would get me. I also had a terrible fear of insects, and I always had a mandatory nightly inspection of closets and would check under the bed before lying down for sleep. Before the age of ten, nightmares involving ravenous hordes of insects plagued my dream state. I would frequently awaken, terrorized, and jump into bed with my parents. As an adult, I rooted out the causes of my bouts with fear, and I found that these fears had stemmed from my prior incarnations.

Because I had persistent feelings of inadequacy, I remember many times as a child wishing for a superpower, like becoming invisible or having super strength. I don't think I was aware of it then, but I did not feel as if I fit in with anyone or in any place. My entire world seemed very unnatural. The children in school seemed immature, and my best friends were older people. My loving soul and lighthearted nature were under assault, even though I was unaware of my spiritual *dis-ease* at the time.

After three years in Santa Barbara, my parents and I moved to Oxnard, in Ventura County, California. This place had a very different energetic quality from Santa Barbara: Ventura had a big-city feel. In middle school, I experienced a pervasive fear I had never yet experienced during the daytime. Minority gangs and surfer gangs, as well as a general sense of viciousness, created waves of fear in the air. It felt like a black cloud, so dense it could be cut with a knife. Most students kept their heads down to avoid drawing negative attention to themselves. Some of the other kids in the neighborhood displayed negativity, picking on each other and fighting.

One day, while walking home from school, a large, mean kid took my books out of my hands and laughed at me. Surprising myself (and him) I tackled him, took my books back, and ran for my life. He tried to catch me, but I made it home. I was always nervous to walk by his house after that. Many but not all the neighborhood kids were mean-spirited. Despite some bad experiences in school, I would whistle while walking to and from school daily. I have always enjoyed whistling.

My favorite person I made friends with during this time was an older janitor named David. I had many conversations with him during my breaks from class. My peers seemed to act like little kids to me: none of them could carry on a conversation, and they seemed to be generally unaware of interactions around them. I was unaware of any of my past incarnations yet, and I did not know why I should feel that way about the other kids. Consequently, I spent a lot of time alone, walking the perimeter of the school. On one such walk, I found a two-foot-long metal bar in the school hedges. I continued looking and found these bars every few feet. I realized that the Hispanic kids were ready for war and had placed these bars strategically in case of a fight. Walking away quickly, I decided not to tell anyone about my find. It seemed that fear loomed everywhere, and I did not think it strange that some cultural groups were more organized than others.

Fortunately, there were a few adult neighbors with whom I could speak, and I also met Warren. He was my age and super cool. We spent a lot of time together, and he taught me how to fish and to play tennis. Like me, Warren seemed to be an older soul, and he soon became my best friend. I never saw him again when my family moved away from Ventura County, and Warren was the only person I ever truly missed, aside from my older brother. Of course, there were a couple of girls I was attracted to from about sixth grade on, but I was way too shy to talk with them.

In 1979, just after I turned thirteen years old, my parents moved us to Lake Tahoe, California. I have lived here ever since, aside from much time spent traveling around the world. South Lake Tahoe is a beautiful mountain town in Northern California on the edge of the Nevada desert. This was a pristine environment to grow up in, with a vast, deep blue mountain lake sitting at an elevation of 6,225 feet. This gigantic lake is surrounded by snowcapped mountain peaks that rise to over ten thousand feet, carpeted by many varieties of evergreen trees. Lake Tahoe is blue and green all summer and white and blue all winter. The winter months are very long.

Except for missing my friend, Warren, who taught me to fish, I was very happy we moved to Lake Tahoe; this was mainly because the fear vibrations I had felt in Ventura did not exist in our new environment. Especially when I started school there, kids held their heads up much more. There were no gangs, and people had a better disposition. It was not until the fear was removed that I realized it had existed in Ventura County. This was when I realized that the generalized fear I felt had been external, not from within me—a huge realization.

There were many kids around my age in my family's new Lake Tahoe neighborhood. Finally, we were staying somewhere permanently, and I could flourish and develop some long-term friendships. Growing up in Tahoe turned out to be fun. I got to fish and swim in the lake, and I learned how to ski. The neighborhood children would get together for games where ten or more kids would participate. We would play tag, football, ride bikes, and walk up the mountains, all running down together.

It was much less fun when I turned fifteen and my dad made me the night shift manager of the motel we had purchased there. Without pay, I was "allowed" to work. Now I spent my days in school and my nights at the motel. In the summers, I actually got paid to clean motel rooms—a meager two dollars per room, earning four to six dollars an hour depending on how fast I worked. As soon as I finished each day, I would go to the beach.

Even though the motel was boring, it provided me a place at night to myself as my parents would retreat to the house we owned. In the following years, the motel turned into the party pad. My friends would come by, we would drink and smoke pot, and then we'd move the furniture and play hacky sack. We spent hours playing hacky together. I also played a lot of hacky sack alone, and I became very proficient at it. From the perspective of my dad's cultural heritage, it was normal to put kids to work. Thus, I learned the motel business: I gained some customer service skills, learned groundskeeping and bookkeeping, and by keeping the motel's sixteen toilets clean, I learned how not to be afraid of getting my hands dirty, which kept me humbly able to clean up after people.

I never liked school, but I made it through by doing just enough work to pass the courses. The fact that I had no supervision, nor anyone to help me understand the material the teachers presented, really did not help. I had no reason to learn, and nobody explained to me why I should do well. A negative self-image that carried over from my past lives, in addition to my mom's negative self-image, plus a pot-smoking habit, made learning in school even less appealing. I threw most of my homework away. It really did not make sense to me to be in school all day and then have to do homework too. The only A's I got were in math, some history classes, and of course, physical education. I really liked American Indian history and mastered those exams easily while still doing the minimum amount of work possible. Being such a slacker, I am not sure how I passed some of those classes, but I never failed a class. One of the few real interests I had was typing class. Woodshop and auto shop seemed like too much work to me. Plus, all the cute girls took typing class. I was typing strictly for the interaction with the girls in the class. Who would have thought then that I would aspire to be a writer? I also really enjoyed volleyball class (again, the female presence was nice) and continued playing volleyball on the community college team for a couple years after high school. I did not actually start dating until I was seventeen. I did not realize until a few years later how dysfunctional I had been. The lack of a proper example of a loving relationship—in addition to being influenced by the cultural variations of a German and Persian mindset—hindered my dating success with American girls. And, of course, my past-life belief systems interfered. It took me a long time to work out my insecurities and to overcome being a wallflower.

We acquired two more small motels, and there was work to be done all the time. So, most of my teen years were spent in the motel and at school. I continued to work—some days and all nights—as a gardener, housecleaner, and manager for my parents in their motel business, all the way through two years of community college in Tahoe. In my two years of college, I studied business as a major and psychology as a minor. I had already decided to follow in my dad's footsteps, immersing myself in the business world.

It was toward the end of those two years, while my parents were on vacation, that I met two Puerto Rican gentlemen who convinced me of the easy money to be made by selling cocaine. Well, that stint lasted just over a month before the police knocked on my door. Luckily, I spent only a few hours in jail. For the whole next year, I had to go to court once a month. This gave me a great peek into the judicial system. The situation ended well. Gracefully, I was released from all charges, and the case was dismissed because of a lack of evidence. The only benefit the coke might have had in my life (besides the money) is that it helped me look outside myself a little more, to become more extraverted, as I was terribly introverted at the time.

This was a traumatic year for me, but it made me flourish, redirecting my attention to health, lifting weights, doing yoga, and understanding the way to make a proper living. It did not strike me until two years later that the dark side had made a bid to shut down my light and to misdirect my life's path.

The dark had also attacked once before the coke incident; I walked into a party a couple of years earlier as a high school senior and met a guy named Bubba. I entered the party, and Bubba addressed me immediately. He proudly said that he worshiped the devil and then told me I had no power. I looked at him for a while, and it turned into a staredown. The people around us tried to get us to stop staring, but we were fully engaged with each other. Approximately two minutes went by, and he made some type of symbol in the air with his hands. I, in turn, followed suit and made a cross in the air in front of him. His eyes watered, and he finally looked away from me, admitting defeat. He immediately bade me come over to the table. I still had no idea what was going on. He picked up a pair of dice and invited me to a game of Mexicali (a.k.a., liar's dice). The game went on for a while, and it was the first time I ever felt psychic. I knew exactly when he was lying about his dice roles. Because we were playing for shots of Everclear (vodka) punch, after about seven drinks, he slumped under the table. I didn't drink any. Again, he admitted defeat and threatened that although I had won the first two battles, he would win the third. This was my first interaction with the dark side.

A year and a half later, I went to a different party. To my surprise, Bubba opened the door and welcomed me in. He looked trim and wore a nice suit and tie. He stood between two beautiful women, who were both all made up. With a big smile, he told me the party was in the back room. It was in the back room that I became acquainted with the two Puerto Rican men who got me into selling cocaine for them. I lived full tilt for a while, nightclubbing and drinking. After less than two months of partying, I was arrested. I got out of the fast lane and never went back to that lifestyle. Likewise, I never saw Bubba again.

I had my first two God realizations two months after my arrest, and then again another year later, after my monthly court visits. I had found faith and trust, smiling in the courtroom, and nobody understood why.

We never know how karma is affecting us, good or bad. Situations that might seem negative at one time might have a very positive outcome, and vice versa.

At age twenty, I spent all my time in the motel and continued to practice martial arts and lift weights. I had been pretty weak before lifting, barely able to lift eighty pounds, but I quickly gained strength. One time, during my tenth repetition of 160 pounds on the bench press, my erector muscles gave out (on the left side between my shoulder blade and the backside of my heart chakra). In constant pain for at least a month, I felt my desire to lift weights immediately dissipate, which ended up being a real gift. Within a month of this spinal injury, I met my first yoga instructor and good friend, Scott. He had just finished his yoga teacher training course and was eager for a student. He had a great perspective on life, and we enjoyed good conversation and music together, especially the Grateful Dead. He got me to enjoy running and taught me many of my first asanas (hatha yoga postures).

With several important lessons behind me, my dad made me an offer to become the leasing owner of the Casa Linda, an eleven-unit motel. Glad to leave my college studies after two years and my past troubles, I fully engaged in this purely monetary pursuit. It was hard work for a while at the motel, but I felt as if I was somebody.

The day that I took over the motel as the leasing owner, Scott took me to my first Grateful Dead show. We drove to San Francisco in my hot little sports car, four hours away. When we arrived at the show, he gave me a tie-dyed T-shirt to put on. I remember how self-conscious this made me feel, as I had become accustomed to wearing suits and ties. I struggled with my ego and later put the shirt on. The show was a wonderful experience. The Grateful Dead opened with the Beatles song, "Hey Jude." Since I had grown up listening to the Beatles on the radio as a child, even in Germany, I was immediately put at ease. I danced all night long and felt great.

The main thing I remember from that concert was the strong sense of acceptance and belonging. I had waited since I was a child for visual recognition from someone, anyone. I found many people at the concert who were not only unafraid to look back at me but who genuinely wanted us to connect with each other. This gave me a feeling of belonging for the first time.

Scott was in my life for several years, after which I never saw him again. Yoga seemed to be the best way to heal my hurt back. A month later, I met my next yoga instructor and lifelong friend, Bob. Bob taught me a lot about God.

Bob, the yoga veteran, manifested so much love and humility that he was able to help me understand the oneness people could have with each other. Although he was lost in alcohol when I met him, he truly knew God and he was able to communicate that. As I saw God in my friend, I learned spiritual consciousness on a whole different level. We had a telepathic connection and shared higher communication. With God's help, I slowly helped him get off drugs and alcohol. However, we still smoked pot together while I taught him how to play hacky sack, a game I'd enjoyed since high school, thanks to my friend Jim.

Bob gave me a copy of the King James Bible, as well as a copy of the Bhagavad Gita. He talked to me about the guru-disciple relationship. Later we dropped a hit of LSD together, and my eyes began to open. With that experience, I gained the awareness that beings that could perceive my thought existed within and outside of the world. Continuously, my life changed, and Bob and I talked about God for hours and years. I became aware of the operation of God on my mind then, and that would continue throughout my life. Bob was a master musician and taught me some music theory, as well as how to interact while playing with other musicians. I learned to play the hand drum and keep time, which helped me work on the attention deficit I had developed as a child. I do not know if it was my parents drinking and smoking that caused it or the fact that nobody helped me develop an attention span by reading to me or allowing me to play an instrument. At age twenty, my creativity flourished, and besides music, I began to write poetry. Bob also shared with me the joy of being in one mind with someone who was not stuck in their ego.

During this time, when I was twenty years old, I practiced yoga daily, and I experimented with LSD and psychedelic mushrooms a couple of times that year. Sitting with deep concentration and meditation, these consciousness-altering substances helped me gain many different spiritual insights. Primarily they helped me overcome my attention deficit, which had posed a challenge to my mental-emotional maturation. The hallucinogens made it possible for me to stay focused on a single subject and ponder it all the way through. They helped me break through the mundane material reality of the world and focus my mind on esoteric spiritual questions about the state of reality, and they helped me look inside. After the first couple of journeys, I felt more alive and noticed my yoga practice going deeper. Music also became much more interesting to me; I could listen longer and more deeply.

The most important realization I had was that all things, experiences, and circumstances were connected and existed to further the purpose God had intended in my life. Living within God's presence, and discovered that my life suddenly had a meaning: I was *wholeness*. All the events of the past had brought me to see this moment of perfection. Creation and evolution together, time coexisting, past and future working together toward God's purpose, in this *now*.

Hallucinogens can be a good tool for growth—a steppingstone—to understanding more of what is possible. It saddens me sometimes to see people partying and wasting the spiritual potential of the mind-altering journey on the external, combining them with alcohol and thereby shutting down the upper chakras (energy centers). This numbs the experience instead of allowing people to look inside themselves.

I am eternally grateful that my guru intervened in my life before I began my hallucinogenic experiences. By grace, I was awakened to God's presence while sober and still the leasing owner of the Casa Linda motel. Soon thereafter, I cut loose from my material bonds to follow God's will for me and went on the road. Releasing money as a primary goal in life, I cut those family ties a few months after my twenty-first birthday.

Disillusioned with the family business and with the greed-centered structure of the world, I felt the need to live a natural, spiritual life. At that time, I not only comprehended the illusion of money but also felt the very real suffering of humankind. However, as I understood it, the prosperity of God's Holy Spirit has always been freely available to everyone. It seems most people were just not using their free will to ask for help, to receive guidance and abundance, and to live in trust. They did not want to refocus the intention of their minds and hearts life away from selfish materialism and toward more selfless charity, compassion, and love. The qualities of love and trust that unify us with *God's will* help us shed fear and worry. When we do not manifest fear and worry in our own lives, we live a purer effortless existence.

I deeply felt in my twenty-first year of life that *spirit* wished for us to enter into and remain within the presence of God, to reclaim our innocence and so our good karma would be naturally attracted to us—a spiritual inheritance.

I quickly gave the Casa Linda motel back to my mom and dad. I also gave them back the car they had given me. I had saved five thousand dollars before I ever took over the motel ownership, and that was what I kept. I bought an old, white 1972 Volkswagen camper van to spend the next couple of years on the road. I traveled to find myself, visiting churches and exploring nature, and I followed the Grateful Dead. The more I allowed myself to become dependent on spirit to inspire, guide, and support me, the less I was concerned with chasing after such worldly illusions as money and material gain. I gave away all my excessive clothes while traveling through Mexico. In Baja, California, I opened my suitcases and let poor people take what they wanted.

I reclaimed the childhood I was deprived of, and I learned how to dance and play. Most importantly, I learned to interact with other people properly. My faith and freedom grew, although self-doubt and worry would constantly try to creep in. Every musical concert I attended, I also bought a ticket for someone else who couldn't afford to go in. The more I gave of my love and shared what I had, the better I felt. It is God's nature to give. I surrendered my vehicle, and I traveled by thumb across the country and back. It was when hitching through New York that I realized people were stuck in their circumstances because of their familiarity with their current situation.

Although my experiences and relations were difficult at times, my life has also come alive with magic, and I almost expect miracles to happen. We continuously get to make good choices, which I do not always make, but I find great learning from my mistakes (which I make more frequently than I like) and allow myself to grow. I have learned that forgiveness for myself is just as important as forgiving others. It is also difficult to forgive others until you realize there is nothing to forgive: this is seeing someone's true wholeness, beyond their circumstances.

A NEW CHAPTER

DURING MY JOURNEYS, I HAVE visited many temples, churches, and sacred sites, and I always feel the *spirit's presence*, whether I'm in the contiguous United States, Hawaii, India, Brazil, or Thailand. I have had many random conversations with people, and I've always wondered how they arrived at their state of awareness and circumstance. I have especially wondered about the life circumstances of poor folks living in the streets. It seems materially poor people believe in their poverty, and this belief is instrumental in keeping them trapped in their poverty and circumstance. They do not, or cannot, believe any other reality could exist for them. While traveling, I've also noticed that poor people frequently gave donations more freely than some of the wealthy people I encountered.

Some people are materially wealthy but spiritually poor, although most people who have material wealth believe in the abundance theory of giving freely and receiving freely. Some did not know any differently, being raised in wealth. At the same time, some people in the street were ridiculously wealthy in spirit, living, and loving, and they still trusted in their lives, even seeing God in others, while outwardly poverty-stricken. It reminds me of the bumper sticker saying: "Not all who wander are lost."

Wandering and camping in different places can really change your perspective. Some of my favorite times as an adult have been in various churches—in religious celebration—or just meeting a stranger. I really enjoy camping out and waking up to the sound of singing birds or ocean waves, as opposed to the sound of a ringing phone while walled inside a building. A note to those who feel they need to receive calls in restaurants and talk real loud: thank you for helping me overcome my judgments.

I was extremely repressed emotionally for a long time; I was so shy around others, especially girls, and would put them up on a pedestal. A negative self-image had almost paralyzed me through my teen years. When I left the family searching for God, after I was first freed, I still had these negative tendencies. It was during these traveling years that I spent much time alone. I learned how to play bongo and conga drums while chanting "Hare Krishna" to keep my mind present. I spent a lot of time writing poetry and, of course, studying yoga. Then I would get high and dance my butt off at the Grateful Dead shows. Opening myself up there in a large crowd felt like I entered a spiritual battleground. Being able to focus on love as I melted with everyone psychically—potentially taking on people's psychic dramas, pain, and delusions—helped force me to open spiritually and hold my center. Learning how to play and dance through this process, I slowly came to embrace our true human oneness, regain empathy, and properly interact with people psychically and emotionally.

Psychotropics were a shortcut to the meditative state. They slowly helped me weed out my pernicious negative self-image by tracing the core roots of the negative thoughts and finding where the projections came from. This introspective process then freed the energy that was stuck, which allowed me to flourish more. I learned to follow thoughts to their end, taking any subject and dissecting it to every avenue possible, whether they be moral constructs or cultural implants. I believe a deep self-inquiry is necessary for anyone to grow.

Traveling all over the United States and Mexico, I continued to release fears and material possessions as I continued to embrace a higher spiritual calling of material worldly poverty. Anything in excess had to leave my life. The world constantly offers us the temptations to amass wealth and gain status, but real wealth and status come from knowing your *eternal soul*. While it is alright to have material wealth and possession, simultaneous awareness of the soul allows us to know we are being taken care of by the universe, which lets us manifest our needs and desires. Being hindered by too much work or excessive entertainment (bars, theaters, sexuality, casinos, and especially *television* and the *internet)*, and fear propaganda can distract us from keeping our minds and hearts in the present moment, where God can be realized.

Without the help of the gurus' grace, as well as psychotropics, which tuned me in to God and allowed me to concentrate and express myself creatively, I would have been unable to make this soul growth.

The dietary and nutritional changes I was making every day—eliminating animal products and eating smaller amounts of food—seemed conducive to my keeping a clear mind and allowing my upper chakra system to stay open.

A drum traveled with me on all my journeys; I played music while singing mantras to keep me flowing spiritually and in the present moment.

When I was twenty-one, my 1972 Volkswagen bus—my home on wheels—afforded me the spontaneous freedom to park and sleep anywhere I wanted in the United States and Mexico. I always prayed for protection and was never hassled by anyone. I have never lacked food, money, or shelter, except by choice.

I have worked here and there, and I find it is gratifying to work doing something I like. Even though I've lived without a ton of money, because of God's grace, I have always had more than enough, and I have even lived like a king. The more time I spent on the road, the less fear I had about money. I was constantly seeing the flow of miracles and how much I was supported by the universe.

I really did not want to become dependent on others though. As free as I had ever been to explore my own spiritual path, I decided to ground my energies back in Tahoe after almost two years of traveling. I chose to do seasonal work that would earn me enough to live while giving me free time in the off-seasons. I sought a job that offered playtime and skiing and would be helpful outside of myself. Thus, I joined the Forest Service, fighting fire.

BACK WITH THE FAMILY

AFTER MUCH FREE TIME AND total freedom, and after I was lifted in the power of love, I returned to my parents' home in Tahoe. I was hoping to find a place to live after working for a while. My parents welcomed me with open arms. My mind and being had changed so much over the last few years, and I really wanted to share the light with everyone. The second day I was home, I began to tell my parents about how I had come to begin loving God. I told them about hearing people's thoughts and feelings. I told them about seeing through the third eye, which allowed me to view people's past lives and see *auras* around their bodies. My parents responded with anger, telling me they wanted me to seek professional help, and assuring me they would pay for a doctor.

Although I was now manifesting much more of my gentle, feminine nature, I fell back into the dysfunctional energies of my youth. I became angry and got into an argument with my dad. Although my father was a good man at heart, he was easily angered. In the middle of the argument, I remembered, I had chosen love as a reality. I immediately stopped arguing and walked away from the dynamic.

In a secluded bedroom, I sat in prayer and meditation. Approximately thirty minutes later, I had fully regained the sense of deep peace within my core and resettled in the deep blue light. Feeling I could put forth a more comprehensive effort, I reapproached my dad where he was sitting alone in the living room. I knelt at his feet and took his hand into mine. I felt his anger rise as I calmly tried to make my point. For the first time in my life, I was able to transform my own anger and respond with love. The power of the spirit of love came through me, and I became supercharged with energy.

With grace, I absorbed the negative energy from my dad and transmuted it, pushing all the love I had through the point of my third eye. I stopped to look at him and realized he was still trying to get angry, so I did it again. I looked again and saw that he was still trying to speak, so again, I pushed all the love that I had at him.

He was suddenly speechless and sat in front of me like a good little boy. I was unaware of what the experience had been for him, but I decided to walk away. The next morning, sitting quietly at breakfast with me, he said, "I saw your third eye yesterday. It opened up three times, and green light poured out."

You cannot imagine my surprise, joy, and relief. Being the smartass that I am, I advised him that perhaps he should go and seek medical help.

Later that afternoon, my mother approached me nervously. Obviously, Dad had shared his mind-blowing experience with her. She asked me with a childish innocence why I hadn't showed my third eye to her, envious I had shared it with my dad. I admitted it was out of my control. We embraced, and I left for work at the ski resort. I now realize that it took three times for my dad to believe what he was seeing and for his ego to release the illusion of anger and accept the presence and reality of love.

After that, neither parent ever hassled me about my beliefs or told me that I was sick—although Dad did believe I should cut my hair and beard and put on a suit to teach God or become a doctor or lawyer. All these options sounded like spiritual death to me. Even though my parents did not hassle me anymore, they never offered me monetary assistance. But they did tell me I always had a place to live.

Even though we lived in snow country, my parents did not invest in ski lessons when I was a child. After returning to Tahoe and working at the ski resort for three winters, I finally became proficient and spent many days flying down the mountain in thankfulness. Everyone I worked with noticed how many people I knew who would come up to me for a hug. I would hug and hold everyone with God's love and soon gained the title "Huggo" from my coworkers. A couple of my coworkers and I had deep spiritual discussions, and it was always interesting what others' perceptions of *spirit* looked like— sometimes fear-based and other times love-based.

Funny enough, while I was working in the Forest Service, I made the mistake of doing a yoga sequence after a long day of work, and everyone called me Gandhi from then on. I told them that Gandhi was too reverent a title for me, but they did not know what I meant. I met some really cool people in the Forest Service, but there were a lot of knuckleheads too. The ski resort and Forest Service were both great jobs that I mostly enjoyed, as I strongly felt we need free time to continue questioning ourselves and grow—which an eight-hour-a-day job really does not allow. I chose ski resorts and fighting fire with the Forest Service, spending the next four years working but still catching concerts in the months between my seasonal jobs.

With my return to Tahoe, I reconnected with my friend, Bob, and we formed a three-piece band with another guy, Dennis, calling ourselves the Cosmic Shuttle Command. We practiced a lot, and we created three hours of original music. After about six months, we took the band out to a local bar and played for more than a hundred people. The crowd loved us, and they danced to the music all night long. Many people even asked if we had an album they could buy. We never played again as the Shuttle Command, but within a month, we formed another band: Bob and I joined two members of the recently disbanded Loafers band, and the five of us became the Cosmic Freeway. We practiced and played regularly. I still remember the first time someone handed me sixty dollars for playing my drum all night: awesome. By 1989, the "Freeway" was a rocking, psychedelic phenomenon.

The town of South Lake Tahoe loved us, and our popularity grew. All of our shows were rocking. We played Grateful Dead cover songs and a variety of originals written by Bob and the other members of the band. Sometimes the music got so focused that we all went into a trance and forgot we still had bodies. When those special songs ended, we could see the bliss in each other and in the crowd. One could feel the unified mind, and time seemed to fly. An hour-long set felt like ten minutes, and it was physically easy.

Other times, if the crowd wasn't dancing and some of us were out of focus, the music would drag, each song took forever, and sometimes, it was even physically painful; my arms would cramp. At times, so much light flooded our shows that we noticed negative people. Hardcore drug users would have to leave the event, as they could not handle the positive vibes and swim in the ocean of love. All the band members understood to some degree the one-minded activity, and there was much love between us.

The band life came to an end for me within a year, though the band continued on for more than ten years. When the drummer quit, we had to wait for the new one to move from the East Coast, so we all took a month off. However, I never returned.

Having received my final Forest Service paycheck, nine hundred dollars in hand, I flew to Hawaii for the month. I ended up staying in Kauai for six months. The guys in the band during that time ended up partying a lot more. They eventually got sponsored by a self-interested lawyer. He took the band in the wrong direction, as he was only profit-oriented. I think they focused on the money and fame after that and lost the spiritual intention we had had at the start.

KAUAI

IN RETROSPECT, I WAS HAPPY to have quit the band, although at the time, it was sad for me to stop playing, as I missed the guys and the scene. I played in many drum circles during the six months I spent on Mama Kauai in 1990, which also helped me release the band. Many people had dropped out of society to live freely on Kauai, among them Hawaiian holy men, some with great spiritual potency.

The higher, clearer energy fields on this living island, along with the many enlightened beings, opened more doorways to spiritual realms. I had the insights at that time that playing music with the proper intention—focusing on God's presence and love—could open these realms. Playing music just for money now felt improper to me.

So many spiritual things happened to me in Kauai, it is hard for me to discuss it all. I felt the *mother* aspect of God so empowered on this island. Even as I arrived there, I felt embraced by a warm feeling of awareness. My spiritual eye opened easily, as I felt less mental interference. I felt my vision lifted into fields of gold that remained at least the first three weeks of my being there. Seeing colorful fields really creates bliss. I quickly met many like-minded people who were also living free.

Upon arriving in Kauai, I hitchhiked from the airport. I was picked up quickly and guided to where I might set up my tent. One thing quickly led to the next in an effortless flow of events, including playing drums on stage and eating a diet of super clean raw foods. I had meetings with many evolved, psychically active beings.

Absolutely, your immediate environment and the people around you make a huge difference on your magnetic field. In public places, we can be relaxed with God but on guard to avoid getting psychic schmutz on us from others.

On Kauai is the only Siva (Shiva) temple in the United States. The temple has some of the cleanest energy anywhere. The monks do a psychic energetic clearing every hour, each day and night; it is the only temple I am aware of that continues with the nighttime practice. The guru there, Sivaya Subramuniyaswami, was born in Oakland, California, in 1927, and grew up at Fallen Leaf Lake, right next to the town where I live (South Lake Tahoe). He went to India with a dance company and joined the Siva order there. When he matured as a swami, he created the first temple in Kauai. He had the idea that humankind was nearly ready for the next thousand years of peace on earth—the coming of a new age. He intended to build the new temple to hold this peaceful energy. It is still in process and almost finished. Subramuniyaswami earned the Nobel Peace Prize and wrote countless books on consciousness, the Saivite (Shaivite) religion, and the ancient Lemurian civilization connection in Kauai.

I was blessed to meet Subramuniyaswami while I was in Kauai. I felt him slap me psychically in the head from thirty feet away. In my mind, I was questioning his spiritual authority; when I felt the slap, I was humbled, and I fell on my face in worship and thankfulness. I found out several years later that his guru had also slapped him upon their first meeting, and Swami was told the slap would be felt all over the Western world.

It was such a blessing to attend temple worship there. I attended almost every week, except when I was hiking in the backcountry valleys. The temple confirmed the importance of the deep practice of religion, meditation, and the practice of union with the *divine* that I had desired to see and understand. This temple also made me realize that although the monks were holding space together with a constant worship practice, they might not be functional in the rest of the world. It seemed to me they had to hide there to keep it together. I began to understand I wanted to be able to function spiritually *and* be in the world—not as a monk but as an expression of God's life.

Upon my return from Kauai to South Lake Tahoe at the age of twenty-four, I was more grounded and focused. I attended and finished a year of massage school training and Reiki energy healing. I began a career in healing, as I had found a way to make money and help people. Soon after graduating from massage school, I went to work in a health club, where I worked full time for several years. I continued to take many classes in various healing styles, mainly focusing on acupressure therapies, where I could continue to channel God's loving energy.

After three years, I was certified to do therapy and went to work for Harrah's Casino in Tahoe. I had easily worked on well over 2,500 bodies. To my own surprise, I had earned approximately four thousand dollars in savings. Keeping a promise I had made to myself years earlier, I flew to India and spent two months traveling from New Delhi to Bangalore and up to Dharamsala, where I was privileged to meet His Holiness the Dalai Lama. By grace, I was allowed to spend three and a half weeks at the feet of my next teacher, Swami Sai Baba. I will return to this topic later.

Upon my return from India, my then-girlfriend and I became pregnant. At the age of twenty-eight, I became a father to a beautiful baby boy. Needing to earn a stable income for my family, I went back to doing massage at the Harrah's Casino health club for another year. That year was the hardest I ever worked. Underpaid and overworked, I finally quit. It was a little scary to trust myself at first, but I boldly opened my own business. I have continued to work hard as a therapist and healer and have been sovereign ever since.

MY FIRST EXPERIENCES IN LIGHT

MY FIRST ALTERNATE EXPERIENCE FROM the norm happened my junior year of high school. The students were playing football during physical education class. As usual, I was getting picked for teams toward the end since I was no great athlete, I was physically insecure, and I had some doubts about my ability to catch and throw.

In the middle of the game, time suddenly froze. Everything began to shimmer, and I somehow knew I could run circles around everyone. It felt as if everyone except for me was moving in slow motion. The ball was thrown, and it too looked slowed down. I ran in front of the receiver and made the easiest interception of my life, running effortlessly for the touchdown. The moment I made the catch, time normalized. This was my first conscious experience of the supernatural. As irregular and fantastic as my experience at that time was, for some reason, I did not give it much thought, and life went on.

The next experience happened in 1984, when I was eighteen years old, at my parents' sixteen-unit motel, the Little Bear Lodge. I was living in room number 15 at that time, a small space. Early in the morning, upon waking, I was struck gently on the top of my head. I saw a golden light move from my head to my feet. While cocooned in that light for perhaps a minute, I felt the deepest peace of my young life. Then the light moved back up my body to the top of my head and was gone. Wow! I knew something very different had just happened to me, but I didn't really know what it was, so I shrugged it off and began my usual workday.

Later that year, to beat the cold Tahoe winter weather, my old high school buddies and I drove down to Carson City, Nevada, to have a game of football at a much lower elevation. It had been quite some time since I had seen these guys, and by that time, I had transformed my physique by lifting weights five days a week. I had not been strong throughout my high school years, but within about a year, I could lift 160 pounds for ten repetitions. Now I was able to intimidate my old friends from school with sheer physical power. It was a nice role reversal to feel strong, as I used to feel intimidated by them. As my ego swelled, I remember thinking of myself like Apollo, the Greek god. I began to strike fear into my friends as I charged the ball, moving the guys around the field effortlessly.

I remember receiving the ball and, before I could run, two people struck my left knee from opposite sides. My knee gave way as my ligaments were abruptly pulled and stretched. Just like that, I was out of the game. For a while, I could only focus on the pain. It is amazing how few beliefs or ideas about reality you can hold onto when you're in real pain. So much for being a Greek god. About a half hour later, I was able to limp away on it, and within a week, I forgot about the injury.

Later in life, I found out while reading *Watch Your Dreams*, by Ann Ree Colton, that the spiritual meaning of a knee injury is humility. A knee injury alerts a person of the need to kneel before the universe. Carrying spiritual or physical power requires much self-control and without humility, there is also no real self-control.

All the little things that happened to me did not mean much. For the most part, they were the same as the experiences of any other young man; I mostly thought of hanging out with my pals and chasing or dreaming of girls. I casually dismissed all the spiritual things that occurred in my life until the next experience.

The next experience, I could not ignore.

THE SHIFT

IF ANYONE HAD ASKED ME at that time, "Are you religious?" I would have said no. Who could have known then that my life was about to take a different turn, completely redirecting my state of physical, spiritual, and mental awareness and faith in God?

At age nineteen, several months after my original knee injury, I was chasing and playing with our pet Doberman when my knee caved in again. As I felt all the bones rotate inside my knee, I fell to the ground. My ligaments were badly sprained, if not torn. In excruciating pain, I tried to stand but could put no weight on it. Hopping to a chair a few feet away, I sat, and the neighbor called out, asking if he could help. The pounding around my knee overwhelmed me. My mom came out of the house saying I had a phone call, and I told her to forget it.

"I need a glass of water," I said.

The pounding in my leg continued, and I thought I would surely throw up. Almost immediately, I heard a voice from above me saying, *No. Divine intervention.* These were words I had never contemplated.

What happened after this is almost beyond words. Suddenly, I felt as if I were looking at the fabric of the universe. It looked like white light, knit together, permeating and underlying everything. It was stunningly beautiful to behold. Behind the light field, I could see I had not moved but was still sitting in my familiar surroundings. Now the rows of shimmering diamonds of brilliant white light, perfectly patterned, overwhelmed. I closed my eyes for a couple of seconds in shock and disbelief. As I reopened my eyes, the vision of light remained. It felt very peaceful. My only thought was that this light must be what knitted the universe together. This time, I knew I wasn't looking through my physical eyes; instead, my vision seemed to come from my forehead or from even higher above my body.

Overwhelmed, I closed my eyes again, fell back, and passed *in*. I say "in" because I did not lose my essential consciousness; rather, I lost awareness of the external reality. It seemed to be flying down a dark tunnel at great speed, with blue and red diamonds, composed of two stacked triangles, rushing by me on both sides. I remained in a state of self-awareness, especially of my face. I still had vision (and maybe hearing and smell), but I had no bodily awareness. I felt ghostlike.

In the distance, I made out a figure on a table. Very faintly, I heard my name being called from behind. My flight slowed. Nearly fifty feet in front of me, I could tell that the figure that lay on the table was the family dog I had been chasing earlier. As I continued to hear my name from behind, I flew backward, and upon returning to my body, the voice progressed from a whisper and became very audible—my mom yelling my name. My body had fallen over in the chair. Mom was lifting my head and trying to pour water in my mouth. She thought I had died, and I could feel her intense emotion.

My immediate desire was to go back into the vision, but she had pulled me out, and the experience was over. As I returned to my body, I never lost the conscious state—from leaving my body to reentering bodily awareness—I stayed present.

Had my mother not called me back at this point, I would have continued my flight and physically died. I believe I was called back by the living (my mom) to begin a new life experience. Some part of me later understood that my karma for this life had ended; this was truly a new beginning.

As my mother called me, I came back to physical awareness. My nose was bleeding, and I got up to walk from the yard into the house. About halfway to the house, I realized I had no pain, and I was walking like nothing had happened. In fact, my knee hadn't hurt since I was immersed in that amazing light.

My young mind was permanently altered by this experience. I thought there should be excruciating pain, but instead, I experienced deep peace, a vision of light, and instantaneous healing of my leg.

What happened the next day blew my mind even further. Our pet Doberman ran out of the house and into the street, where he was run over by a truck and instantly killed. The dog had been the figure in the vision. I had been given the vision the day before by … they? God? Whatever it was, it knew beforehand that the dog was going to die. This really confused my concept of the space-time relationship and made me wonder: Was past, present, or future real? I was also bewildered by the knowledge that something or someone knew what was going to happened before it occurred.

Now, I could not ignore the experience. This spurred me to contemplate reality anew. As my young mind reeled, I questioned all things. I wanted to know how the universe worked, and slowly, the answers came.

After the injury experience, I sensed that my karma had ended for this incarnation and a new dharma (life purpose) was emerging. At the time of the injury, I did not know that by coming into contact with the *light*, I had also touched my *soul history*. I had connected my varied lives, and I would now work on the karma from previous and future incarnations. Over the next twenty years, on perhaps ten occasions in different ways, some of my past lives would be revealed to me. These past life memories were rarely revealed strictly for empowerment; usually, there were leftover personality flaws from those past incarnations—incorrect beliefs about life that still needed to be cleared so they did not become a current issue. Additionally, past lives with unfinished outcomes, such as dying before finishing what I wanted to complete, needed to be processed. However, a couple of past lives were indeed very empowering.

A FEW MONTHS LATER ...

I GREW UP WITH AN awareness of martial arts. From the age of five or six, my older brother taught me the basics of karate: hits, kicks, falling, and stances. He is more than nine years older, and I looked up to him as a teacher. He had taken years of classes in Germany and continued in the States with different styles, including Shotokan karate and kickboxing. So, even though I grew up sparring with him, and later with different people, I had no formal martial arts training and never held a belt.

Around the age of twenty, after my first profound light experience, Chris, one of my best friends since eighth grade, had just earned his black belt. He came over to tell me the news. We sparred a little. Of course, I knew he was a really good martial artist, and he probably could have picked me apart, but I just happened to be faster, and it bothered him. I think he really did not want to hurt me.

The next day, I was at the motel I managed, sitting with my friend Lewis, smoking a joint. Chris brought another new black belt over: his buddy, Dave—a person I was acquainted with and liked but did not know well. He was a lot taller and stronger than I was, and he was well-studied.

Chris invited me to spar with his friend—obviously to teach me a lesson and to humble my ego. Of course, a real martial artist would never have done this, but they went so far as to even bring sparring gloves. Super intimidated, I was thinking no but instead said yes to the match. As we stepped out to the lawn, the match began. I still thought it was for fun, but then, my opponent attacked with a vicious sidekick, aimed at my head. Leaning back as far as I could, I ducked the kick, but it glanced my forehead.

Though I was shocked at the suddenness of such aggression, to my surprise, I lunged forward and connected a left-right fist combo to his jaw. He was clearly dazed, but he actually shook off the blows and moved toward me quickly. To my dismay, I could see his anger growing as he released a multitude of kicks and punches in my direction. I retreated and managed to evade his attacks. He became enraged, and I think I giggled at his anger as I kept a level head. I never became angry while sparring. There was no reason for me to be mad at this person; mostly, I was scared, and I continued to back away.

Backing up further, unaware I had reached a short brick wall, I lost my balance and began to fall backward. As my arms flew up in the air to catch my balance, I felt his fist hit me in the stomach! I felt the blow, but there was no pain. I was just shocked by his attack. I remember thinking, *That wasn't fair.* He had backed up a few feet. All I remember is taking one or two steps forward to attack, and then my vision completely blacked out. I have absolutely no idea what happened then, except for the eyewitness account of my good friend, Lewis, who was also a martial artist.

My vision returned in the air, as I was landing. Internally, I was feeling a warrior's perspective, preparing to land in a perfect martial art form—ready to move on my opponent to attack—when I realized the match was over.

My opponent sat on the ground, knocked out. His eyes were going in different directions, and the side of his face was bloody. He was completely unresponsive. Chris immediately sat down to attend to him.

My friend Lewis ran up to me with joy for my win. He said, "I always knew you were great." I left Chris and Dave outside and invited Lewis come into the house to ask him what had just occurred. He told me I had jumped about ten feet toward Dave through the air and landed some type of hooking heel kick to my opponent's head. That one kick ended the match immediately. I didn't even know I was capable of a jumping kick like that.

Looking at the person, I had just hurt stirred a deep semse of compassion in me. It hurt me emotionally to have caused someone pain. After everyone left, I fell into deep prayers to God to never again be anyone's negative karma. I remember saying in my prayers that if God needed me to fight mental battles for Him, I would, but I never wanted to fight anyone physically again. Soon thereafter, I gave away my martial arts toys—my nunchucks, sword, and throwing stars—and I never sparred again, although I continued to lift weights.

I certainly experienced a different state of awareness during the sparring match, one which transcended memory. Now I chose to believe that while I had previously merged into the *white light* (i.e., the state of non-dualistic reality where the mind is at rest), my past lives converged and became one life. It seems the skills I had developed in previous incarnations were naturally with me in my time of need. Or had the spirit just taken me over to deliver Dave his karma?

AWAKENING IN SAMADHI

AFTER LEARNING LESSONS FROM MY weightlifting and knee injuries, Bob helped me to experience the egoless state and the fact of God's *eternal presence*, which exists when we can really stay in the present moment. He introduced me to the Self-Realization Fellowship lineage of masters: the Lord Krishna and the Lord Jesus, followed by Mahavatar Babaji, Sri Lahiri Mahasaya, Sri Yukteswar, and Swami Paramahansa Yogananda—my guru—who awakened me from my dream state. Now, I believe the spirit of the divine always gives us what we really need once we have chosen the path.

Bob was the only individual at that time of my life (in the 1980s) who was hyper-conscious enough to understand and fully appreciate the changes I was to experience over the next several years. I could recognize God in Bob, even if he did not perceive it in himself at the time. He gave me the book *Autobiography of a Yogi*, by Paramahansa Yogananda. As I read about this master's spiritual life and his encounters of the spiritual beings he met on his journey toward God, I was truly inspired. We can practice yoga for years before knowing what union is before we begin to live the truth and progress up the spiritual ladder. Most people make it to that ladder of enlightenment and think they have arrived, when in reality, they are only on the first step.

While I was still working at my parents' motel at age nineteen, the great guru Paramahansa Yogananda addressed me during my dream state. It was a few months after I had read his book.

He stood in front of me, larger than life. He spoke with me through telepathy, as his lips did not move. He pointed at my body lying asleep in bed and made me realize I was standing in front of him, conscious in mind yet unconscious in body! Realizing this truth, he said, "Now you understand."

I bowed and humbled myself before the living master. As I bowed, I saw a train track in front of me, the same train track I would recognize and cross in India some seven years later. As I rose back up to see him, he was gone, although an incredible golden light remained that filled my vision and being. I felt, for the first time, complete bliss with God's presence.

I never lost my waking conscious state even though I had left my body. I opened my physical eyes to see the golden light of God's presence still filling my bedroom. This was the first time I experienced Samadhi: the God-enlightened state of bliss. It was a timeless experience, and I have no idea how long I lay there before I got up and started my new day.

This was the first time in my life I felt enveloped in the *radiant presence of God*, who is both intimate within our hearts and our minds. This was when my guru-disciple relationship began to flourish, although I had never met the man. Even though we were not near physically, we had a mental and emotional connection that eliminated the distance between us.

My guru would visit me several times more, but only during my waking state. There were several visits at intermittent times over the next six years. During this time, my guru first advised me to change my diet, not for any worldly reason but to be able to see the higher planes, to see auras, and also to feel light physically.

One time in the meditation garden at Harbin Hot Springs in Northern California, I saw my guru descend right before me from about twenty feet above. I just remember leaning into the right side of my head and blissing out, although nothing was said. Another time in Kauai, I was sitting in a house, chanting, "Hare Krishna." I chanted for well over an hour with another devoted friend.

As I came out of the chant in complete mental silence, I began witnessing my friend. I noticed that even though he was chanting, he was not clear; he was lost. Immediately after this realization, Yogananda appeared again in front of me, smiling. Then I was out of body with him, as my position in the room had changed, and the guru and I were on either side of my friend. We spun around him quickly, together creating a type of vortex, and then I was back in my body. The guru vanished, and my friend looked present and clear. We smiled at each other, but I never told him about the experience. This was the first time I felt included, with God allowing me to help someone else instead of just being helped. I had helped people with energy or psychic healing before but not from my *light body* or from an out-of-body perspective. When we stopped chanting, I enjoyed the peace of a thought-free mind, and I sat in the golden light.

DREAMTIME GROWTH

AFTER THE GURU FIRST INTERVENED, my dreamtime awareness began to increase. For the next year, I was frequently in a lucid dream state. I will share a couple of the first occasions.

One dream happened in familiar surroundings when I had just turned twenty years old. I was at the front desk of the motel. As I stood behind the counter, I saw him approach through the window: a Hell's Angels kind of biker wearing all black. As he came to the open door, I saw a large knife in his hand. Immediately as the danger approached, I looked up and into the *divine light* through my spiritual eye, feeling God's presence. My fear extinguished. Taking another look at the man, the knife was gone, and he was handing me flowers.

In another lucid dream, I was walking toward my car when I noticed two Doberman pinschers were in my way, approaching and growling, cutting me off from my vehicle. Again, I looked up into the spiritual eye at the *divine presence*, and as I overcame my fears, the dogs lay at my feet.

Soon I had several more experiences of overcoming fear during the dream state, which transitioned from the dreamscape activity to overcoming fears in my waking life. Gradually, I became more positive and trusting in my own reality. Finally, as an adult, the insight of overcoming fears made more sense, as I recognized how much fear paralyzes our spirit.

ASTRAL PROJECTIONS

FOR A COUPLE OF MONTHS, while I was the motel manager, I began inducing out-of-body projections during daylight hours. After a long morning of sun-gazing meditation, I would go back indoors and lie down. Eventually, I would pop right out of my body. During these projections, I could not predict where I was going. They gave me the insight that multiple dimensions existed.

As I lay down, my eyes rolled up, and I would usually project to familiar surroundings. The last time I intentionally projected, I exited my body, stood up, and found myself in the living room of my apartment. There were several people I did not know sitting around and having a conversation next to the empty shell of my body. Listening to their conversation and its lack of interesting content, I quickly became bored and turned to the kitchen.

I walked in my astral body toward the kitchen and looked out the window there, perceiving an approximately eight-inch tall by six-inch-wide translucent white heart. As I stared at it, its energy pulsated and filled my own heart with energy—a lot of energy. The translucent white heart gave me a great sensation of fullness and love.

The sensation made me want to fly; I even questioned my ability to do so. As I reached my arms forward and lunged, I gently floated to the ground like a feather.

The moment I touched the ground, my senses shifted, and I was back in my body on my back on the sofa. Though I was in my body, I was paralyzed. My eyes would not open, and I couldn't move my arms or any part of my body. Noticing a loud sound of rushing waters behind me, I decided to somehow add energy toward the sound, pushing from my medulla center at the top of my cervical spine. The noise got so loud it sounded like a thousand waterfalls, and I felt my physical body wanting to lift.

Terrified and overwhelmed, I prayed for the experience to stop, and within a few moments, it did. I was able to open my eyes, but for a while, I was motionless in shock, contemplating what had just happened. I believe my desire to fly in the astral plane had actively transferred to my physical body, but I was not yet ready for that experience. The sound of rushing water scared me. It had been so loud, feeling as if the whole universe were coming into me.

Having experienced so many occasions now where my consciousness existed apart from my body, I began to wonder. These experiences sparked a deep contemplation of what was real and what was not. My fears stopped me from investigating or testing the limits of these abilities any further. It felt as if I would have eventually levitated if I had continued on this path. I stopped wanting to project and leave my body, stopped wanting to fly. However, I continued practicing meditation. Realizing slowly but surely that we, humankind, were not just physical beings spurred me to further seek the truth about reality and God.

As I continued a daily yoga practice with my friends, I gained more insight. After about one month of practicing, during the relaxation at the end of one practice, I saw an incredible display of golden light on the ceiling and in the room. I think this was one of my first in-body experiences of the *light*. Later on, with much more practice, the realization hit me that this was my own aura emerging. The light was coming out of me during a deeply concentrated but relaxed state.

With all these experiences, I could no longer be in the world. I soon would be released from earthly duties to simplify my life. Slowly, I let go of any concerns about earning money or creating relationships to follow God's will for me. I tried to let go of the world.

MY LORD

PEOPLE ARE TOLD TO BELIEVE blindly in Jesus. Am I really supposed to believe in someone who was here two thousand years ago? I couldn't really believe in Christ even though I had tried—until it happened.

A couple months after traveling to Mexico in my Volkswagen Bus in 1988, I returned to attend a small regional Rainbow Gathering in Big Sur, California. The Rainbow Family of Living Light was started by six "hippies" who were dedicated to God in the 1960s. These annual gatherings continue to this day, as the group prays for world peace every Fourth of July. Today, more than thirty thousand people gather from the first to the seventh of the month in a different location every year. The purpose is to come together in silence on the morning of July 4 to pray for world peace, from 7:00 a.m. to about 1:00 p.m.

Sitting with thirty or forty thousand individuals in meditation to spread light is quite an experience, all I can say is, "Shift Happens." I experienced many energetic shifts while at these wonderful gatherings, where everyone is fed by huge kitchens, and people give their time to pitch in wherever they can.

There are only three rules at these gatherings: no guns, no money, and no alcohol. You can be naked and get as high or low as you want without being judged. It is an emotionally supportive, family-oriented scenario.

In my continuing struggle to release all worldly possessions and keep my mind focused on God's love, after giving away my suitcase of clothes, I now gave my tent to a needy hippie at the gathering, who turned out to be one of the very early participants. It felt so good to give.

It was April, 1988, a month before my twenty-second birthday. I had just arrived at the Rainbow Gathering after a long drive. It was a small gathering, deep in the woods, with only about five hundred people gathered. We were relaxing in a circle of ten men around a campfire there when I first saw Him.

The group of men were discussing spiritual concepts, such as enlightenment, and sustainable agriculture. Mostly, I listened, as I was younger than everyone else. Suddenly, my eyes lifted above everyone's head, and all the people disappeared from view. He pierced through the clouds of my perception. From a distance, Jesus flew toward me on a golden cross, dressed in white flowing gowns, until he came close enough and I saw his face. My attention was drawn to a tear from his left eye rolling down his check. My consciousness was projected forward as I left my body and flew into the tear.

This was my first contact with my *older brother*, Jesus. To be clear, I was very sober and had been for a long time. I have no idea what happened next, because I had passed out, overwhelmed by the experience. I came back to my body hours later, awakening in the fetal position. The fire was out. All the people had gone. I had a vivid memory of the experience, but it was definitely over. Cold and shocked, I retired to my van to sleep. Although there was no other obvious communication from him, the unshakeable feeling I had been welcomed back into the spiritual family permeated my being.

MY TWENTY-SECOND
BIRTHDAY PRESENT

THE NEXT BIG SHIFT IN my young awareness occurred on my twenty-second birthday. I was camping at Lyons Canyon in Ojai, California, spending a couple of nights there with four others, all folks who were part of the counterculture from the hippie community whom I had been privileged to meet while traveling in Santa Barbara. We all decided to trip together and took a few tabs of LSD.

As the journey began, I noticed that some people were lost in their heads while others maintained an awareness of God. This is when the benefit of being in a spiritually aware group while tripping became obvious to me. As the LSD tapped us in to ourselves, the energy level rose and things got more intense. I could feel my cells vibrating. I had to make the effort to stay in the moment, as every thought became actualized and interactive.

There was an attractive young woman in the group. She was already with someone else, but I felt a connection with her. As I had spent the last year practicing celibacy, I focused on ignoring her energy. Getting higher and higher on the hallucinogens, she hit my lower chakras with an energy that felt strange. Now my sexually stimulated energy felt like a separate creature to me, living right at my perineum. It took my attention away from my mental and spiritual awareness. The need to calm this creature came to the forefront of my mind. Since I was young, I had always been able to control that function of my body and with a couple of seconds of focus, could make my erection relax.

It took all my mental energy to focus, to calm what felt like a creature separate from my true spiritual focus. As I did not realize sexuality and spirituality could coexist, I continued with deep breath and focused completely on the low energy centers in my body. I kept relaxing my lower chakras more and more, mentally, physically and emotionally. It took more than an hour of focus before the creature went completely silent and I was calmed.

Now connected to the root of my being, I perceived that a spiritual anointing had occurred. In this deep stillness, I felt three fluid drops, each several seconds apart, rising up my spine. I felt each drop come from the base of the spine, flowing up the spine into my medulla oblongata at the back of my head and then continuing up the back of my head to the center-top of my head.

As I felt each drop of liquid light touch the top of my crown, the fluid dispersed and expanded, giving me a sense of even deeper peace, expansion, and relaxation. Later, I learned that the field of human anatomy maintains the spine stops at the medulla and does not continue up. My own experience contrasts with previous Western medical knowledge, as I witnessed this connection firsthand. During lectures in India years later, Swami Sai Baba explained and confirmed my experience of the connection of the base of the spine to the top of the crown, both physically and energetically. He also said that Earth is the only planet where this evolutionary jump, and the *ascension* process, was even possible.

Around this time, I was also realizing people had different levels of spiritual awareness due to varied levels of spiritual development, evident in their nervous systems. Through much meditation, we can advance our nervous systems to connect with higher dimensions more easily.

As the—I suppose—*cerebral spinal fluid* melted into my brain, my visual perception completely changed; the heavens opened into beautiful color fields. Mentally and visually, this was deepest state of peace and stillness I had ever experienced. I perceived the Holy Spirit's guidance, and I actually saw sound moving as a combination of color and vibration. This may be the most profound vision I have ever experienced. The vibrations moved from high in the visual field downwards as the sound vibration continued to change several times as it descended. To my further surprise, the vibration then touched the crown of one of the people in the group. The sound vibrations changed once more and then came out of the person as words. I have no idea what he said; my mind was spinning at my new realization of God's creation. I remembered my guru's definition of the Holy Trinity: Tat, Sat, and Aum (the Sanskrit words). God the Son (Tat) lives within vibratory creation; God the Father (Sat) lives beyond vibratory creation; and God the Holy Spirit (Aum) moves all creation through vibration and is the only doer of all actions in the world.

At this moment of seeing creation and realizing the Holy Spirit, it became abundantly clear to me that *spirit* could move us via sound vibrations, if we chose to be open to it.

Most people in the group were completely distracted, their minds way too busy to see or to hear the spiritual guidance that's always available. And of course, there is always the spiritual properness, which suggests *spirit* would not interfere with their "free will."

As I realized I could possibly be interfering with God's goodwill with my everyday thoughts and desires, I was overwhelmed by my own negative self-image. It would have been really nice at this point to feel I was whole and to feel at one with what I perceived (*this knowing is absolutely everyone's birthright, or soul inheritance*). My soul was still holding a lot of guilt, and since I really had not wronged anyone else in this lifetime, I assumed it was from past life activities (which I wasn't yet privileged to know about).

In this moment I remembered a Bible verse that says the devil was to be bound for a thousand years. Seeing how our thoughts could be separating us from God, I took on that negative self-image of myself as this separate ego. I never wanted to interfere with creation again. Praying so deeply, I asked to be bound, even if it meant I should be bound right here in Lyons Canyon, for the next thousand years. I tried to lay down my life for the good of the whole.

I made the effort to surrender into the *presence*, looking into and projecting out through my third eye. At first there was peace, and then my mind was flooded with thought. Fighting for pure consciousness, free from the thoughts that clouded my spiritual vision, I continued redirecting my attention into my spiritual eye to surrender into God.

Again and again, I heard the voice of my aunt saying, "Who are the people you're going camping with?" Every possible fear theme variation came: fear of the other people, sexual fears, and many self-doubts, as if my personal demons knew exactly what would deter me from my effort.

Being thwarted from my most intense desire to be with God was frustrating. I halted my thought once more. For the third time, I redirected my spiritual intention and vision toward *spirit*. This time, it was effortless. The peace took me. I was sitting in the lotus posture, bent forward and bowing.

Immediately realizing my spiritual body had turned upward, I was now facing up toward the sky while my physical body faced into the ground. I saw the sky, and two very large cellar-like wooden doors closing me in. The thought of being bound for a thousand years did not deter my meditative efforts. As I watched the doors close, the prospect of being sealed in made me happy, smiling, ever thankful for God's acceptance. I completely lost consciousness, having no idea where I went or for how long I was gone. I am guessing I was only out for an hour or maybe a minute—luckily not a thousand years.

As my consciousness and body awareness returned, I found myself still bent forward in lotus position. The perception of subtle white light permeated my being, inside and out. Lifting my head and rising slowly, I felt myself come up, feeling snakelike as I rose. Sitting upright, the same woman in the group stood before me; she was dressed all in white and held a flower in her hand. She touched it to my forehead and said, "You are pure." What a relief! I really needed that statement to have an outer confirmation of this most intense inner experience and to ease me back into my body.

For the next few days, I moved within the Holy Spirit, humbled, empowered, and relaxed, feeling the perfection of every action, the *divine* energy coursing through me. As I was no longer stuck in any thought patterns, my vision just faced outward. A true feeling of divinity imbued my being and permeated my consciousness. The peace and truth continued long after the hallucinogens wore off. Perhaps for the first time since my childhood, I felt whole and knew I wasn't alone.

I believe Jesus said, "Knock and it will be opened. Ask and you will receive." My diligence and intense focus had paid off. This lasted for a while, at least until more karmic work presented itself.

PAST LIFE DREAM HEALING

AS A CHILD I HAD many recurring nightmares, mostly about insects. In fact, from the time I was six years old, I performed a nightly insect check before going to sleep, checking the closet and under the bed before the lights went out. In my dreams, on occasion, hundreds of various insects would be crawling toward me, up the blankets of my bed. Many nights I awoke terrified, and I'd run to my parents' room and climb into bed with them. These dreams had stopped somewhere around the age of nine, but I was still scared of the dark. I had forgotten about these nightmares until, as an adult, I awoke from the same dream in the middle of the night in the Dead concert parking lot. Six of us had rented a motorhome for the show, and we all had a little corner to sleep in.

As I woke from the dream, still in fear, my friend Sherrie also sat up a few feet away from me. We looked at each other for a few seconds and went back to sleep. The next morning at breakfast we discussed our dreams. It turns out she had had the exact same nightmare about insects simultaneously. Creepy!

In our group, my friend Gavin was a channel for a spirit he called Victoria. I really wasn't sure about anybody channeling another spirit, but Gavin agreed to channel Victoria so we might figure out what had happened to us. We gave it a go. Victoria helped us remember a lifetime in Egypt when Sherrie and I were members of a priestly order. She suggested it was at the time of Pharaoh's death. The Egyptians believed that many of the servants and priests needed to be there at his death in order to serve him on the other side. We were buried alive in his tomb under the pyramid; a dark and excruciatingly slow death ensued, devoid of food, water, or air. Hundreds of insects feasted on our dying bodies. I could really feel that lifetime. We thanked Victoria for solving the mystery (I never had that nightmare again).

I believe that memory opened a time rift between all of my lifetimes. Because I had already turned back to God by this time and felt solid, I was able to deal with it. When other life streams reveal themselves to me, I reexperience the personality of that incarnation. It can be temporarily confusing as to which life I am living in. Sometimes, I even visually witness people as they looked during the period of the past life I'm experiencing.

The guilt of having influenced so many people, as a priest in Egypt, to worship Pharaoh instead of the one God, weighed heavily on my mind. It took at least a week to come to terms with this memory and forgive myself. As more and more memories came after this gateway experience of remembering my former lives, my state of awareness took another permanent change, and life became larger.

After talking with Victoria, I sat outside of the motorhome at the Dead concert, my state of perception altered. My ultimate understanding what those nightmares meant seemed to open another time rift: every fifth or sixth person who walked by me suddenly looked Egyptian. I could see the garb they had worn in Ancient Egypt, and many wore thick black eye makeup. I wondered why I was seeing random Egyptians in my visual field. I realized obviously not everyone incarnated now had been in Egypt in that period; nor did they carry the specific karma of Ancient Egypt.

Suddenly, I found myself out of body sitting high on a cloud. Again, I was completely sober at the time. Two other Egyptian figures sat next to me on the cloud, and we were wearing all white, with white headdresses. I exchanged no words with them. It felt like a time warp, as I remembered beliefs we had held in those ancient days about the state of the world, hierarchies, and people's roles. I found that my current awareness did not agree with some of those past-life belief systems. Something shifted in me in that moment: I realized we all agree on perceptions and beliefs, which is what makes them real. However, our perceptions continue to change and evolve.

We can change our past and heal the karma by finding the root of our thought structures or beliefs and changing them at the source. With love and forgiveness of the self and others, healing everything becomes possible. Feeling, as opposed to thinking, is a more natural state of experiencing our everyday awareness. Thought, even if it is just a thought impulse, is always a precursor to emotional response. As we become aware of this emotional energy, we can ride these emotional waves back to the source of the thought that created them. This is the only true healing. Then we may have conscious responses to any input instead of emotional responses. We can heal ourselves, each other, and the world so we may return to love.

Emotional responses throw people off their center, and people do not listen or heal while there are still trapped emotions stuck in their body-mind. The need to heal these emotions must be recognized by the people who still hold these self-limiting fears in their being, individually and socially, for us to progress as a whole.

MY YOGA PRACTICES

YOGA MEANS "UNION" IN SANSKRIT.

Yoga has many avenues of expression and offers many routes to reach a state of spiritual union within yourself. When Jesus says, "Take my yolk upon you," he is suggesting to take up his union with the divine. This is the act of merging into these yet unseen fields of energy accessible by the spiritual eye in order to see, feel, and express God—and to learn through this grace. Only an enlightened *master* can give this dispensation of grace. There are many paths of practice, and it can take many years and many lifetimes. The only shortcut to pure consciousness or enlightenment is by the intervention of a guru's grace so that God may be revealed! This intervention can come from whomever your guru might be in this incarnation.

Bhakti yoga, the practice of love and service to others to experience union with the divine, does not necessarily include any exercise. Practicing Kundalini yoga raises the dormant spinal energies that are stuck at the base of the spine. Kriya yoga is deep meditation, which includes sound vibrations and requires an initiation by a master from the Self-Realization Fellowship, or SRF.

I teach hatha yoga, which builds and prepares the circuitry in your body to receive and hold more and more spiritual energies, just as a light bulb can hold varying wattages. You could think of it as a body bulb.

Hatha yoga, with ample meditation but also with much physical movement and stretching, allows the practitioner a healthy alignment of bones, muscles, and ligaments. The deep stretches allow the meridian systems to open and energy to flow, along with the breath, or pranayama, which brings the cosmic life force into the body-mind. *Prana* means life, and *yama* means death, both of which coexist in the breath.

There are many other forms of yogic expression. Worship of the *mother,* or the female aspect of God, frequently includes the five elements of earth, water, fire, air, and ether. In Ashtanga yoga, which is hardcore hatha that provides good exercise and helps you sweat it out, one can include breath of fire, or sound breathing, to really energize the practice.

Also, the newer Bikram (hot) yoga style, which is now very popular, where the room is heated to more than 100 degrees Fahrenheit, does increase flexibility. Personally, however, I don't enjoy it. It can open the body faster than it needs to open up, and it can be way too difficult for beginners, possibly causing injury. Plus, in most cases, with the doors closed to retain heat in the room, oxygen can become sparse, which is counterproductive, as one of the main reasons to do yoga is to oxygenate the body. However, I invite you to try it for yourself and form your own opinion. Many people like it.

Many Tibetans and Hindu cultures use mantras in their yogic practice, which are repetitions of the holy names of God or the divine incarnations of God. Each mantra used may invoke a slightly different energy of the divine. For example, "Aum Namah Shivaya," asks for union with the *Absolute*—just God—while "Aum Namo Sri Ganesh Sai Namo" may be a request for health or money. Also, "Om Tare Tu Tare Ture So ha" asks for all humankind to be lifted into divine awareness. There are also simple mantras, such as "So ham," which means, "I Am That," affirming our state of divine union. There are countless yoga practices and mantras for aspiring yogis and yoginis to choose from, which train the mind to stay in this now moment. With much study and trial, you will see what is right for you and develop your own practice.

At the age of nineteen, I learned the yoga practice quickly, and I loved how it made me feel. It allowed me to recapture the natural bliss of my early childhood. My current practice includes hatha, bhakti, ashtanga, pranayama, and many mantras. *Prana* is the same as Chi, Reiki, or Manna, depending on the culture: it is all life-force energy.

Through our breath during meditation, we allow this subtle life force energy to flow through our body. Prana is considered to be like a fountain of youth. With God's blessing, the energies shift to the *crown chakra* and then flow down to the body. Light energy permeates us physically and also feeds our etheric body and soul.

Whenever opening the crown chakra, be sure to open the *base chakra* at the same time, to avoid spending lifetimes lost in the ethers. Also, no matter what, the end goal is the *heart*. The heart is actually your conscious feeling mind.

After only one month of practicing hatha yoga, at the end of my routine, during a deep relaxation pose on my backside, I witnessed *golden light* pulsating and playing on the ceiling of my living room. This was the first time I saw this blissful golden light. Over the next months and years, it turned blue, then gold and blue, then purple and gold, purple and green, as God continuously kept adjusting my frequencies. Then years later, I reached my spiritual goal and merged into the *white light*, at my guru's feet in India (this is covered in detail later in the book). Now most of my meditations are bathed in deep blue light whenever I am feeling the *loving presence*.

I have now practiced yoga for more than thirty years, and it has been a huge blessing in my life. I have really enjoyed teaching, but mostly learning, during these sessions. Usually, if I do not make conscious contact for a while via yoga or meditation, everything is more difficult, and my stress grows. Yoga is one of the few forms of exercise that incorporate relaxation into the routine.

There are three different levels of a healthy mind's conscious activity: *contemplation*, which can be thinking about life, a flower, God, your state of reality, or anything; *concentration*, or a one-hundred-percent focus on any subject; and *meditation*, which is one-hundred-percent concentration on God and nothing else. If you do not yet know God, then one should practice cultivating peace, listening, breathing, and stilling our thoughts. If you do know God, then we are cultivating peace, breathing, and stilling our thoughts while becoming able to receive direct knowledge and guidance.

Although I get lazy with the routine of my physical practice of yoga, very few days have passed without meditation in my life. When we are meditating, we are practicing yoga. The physical practice just keeps the muscles, bones, and mind integrated. I believe the more fluid the body is, the more fluid your mind can be. The older I get, the more childlike I feel, and it is just a matter of practicing and remembering. It becomes more obvious to me that I have a restless mind and really need to work on it to hold stillness.

Even though I know God is always present, as us, it is incredibly easy to forget. We get stressed out as we are bombarded by the world's information. Sometimes the people closest to us affect us the most, as we also feel their stresses. What helps me to keep peace in my life is retreating into meditation and making an effort to consciously stay connected with God daily, because then, I am reminded and uplifted. Meditation is the act of re-*member*ing that we are a *member* of the universe, here to trust and enjoy life. Accepting the ability to play, we let go of a worrying, churning mind. The things we worry about 99 percent of the time are not within our control anyway. The more I meditate, the more sensitive I become to others' feelings. Some people think meditation is a form of escape; I have even noticed that it is sometimes used incorrectly as a death wish. But a true state of meditation is life, the desire for consciousness and connectivity. Meditation truly engenders a desire toward serving and helping others, and helps with the ability to forgive others, and especially forgive oneself.

One of my favorite teachers, Swami Sai Baba, said, "Wake God up every morning." This statement suggests that we lose consciousness when we go to sleep, and we have to reestablish this contact daily.

Hinduism holds the belief that God rests in infinite peace. Only when we make that effort for connection can *unity* become possible. The formless, omnipresent part of God, *spirit*, is really happy to be embodied by us through prayer and through play. As the *spirit's* essence is love, it would be hurt by all the negative energies when we are doing hurtful or selfish things that cause pain for ourselves or others.

God will break all the karmic laws for love—for your love! The truth shall set you free, and a new life begins for the *seekers*. Joining into your own soul is a loving marriage and a renewed trust in your life. With much practice, you will begin to hear the angels speaking with you. There are many orders of angels, and there are books about them if you would like to know more. They express God's word in different dimensions. Some angels know what to do, and others wait for your commands and prayers.

As you learn to feel, you will feel everyone's emotions, but you will be able to hold your own loving center in peace. Thus, if we are making conscious contact, as we maintain our upper centers of consciousness, we are open, and we are not dwelling in one of the lower thought centers. Once you have established a strong meditation practice, interacting with others will become more effortless.

At any time of day when I invest time in calming my mind and body, I realize they are the same thing. As I free my body through my yoga practice or through certain types of physical therapy, I relax physically and mentally. When I can receive this gift of truly relaxed communion, it releases all anxiety and physical pain. Our cells are detoxed by the *light*, and as we begin to release trapped emotions and traumas from current and past existence, we become pain-free.

Medical doctors frequently name different causes of illness. However, spiritually, every disharmony is really caused by *dis-ease*, mentally, physically, and emotionally. The tensions of existence are stored in our bones and tissues; our muscular structures hold more current issues, while our bones are working out the older negative karma. Should pain arise, I'm able to release it. It takes a long time—sometimes years—but frequently, the pain will release instantly once I recognize the cause of the tension. Throughout my l, ife I have been blessed to receive a lot of help from spirits, doctors, and healers in keeping my mind and body harmonized, and I deeply appreciate it all. The mind is what stays after the body falls away. The body and heart hold your ability to receive spiritual teaching; the body is your learning tool.

My body is storing the information of my daily existence in my tissues, muscles, organs, and bones. The ability to release such body memories at will arises through communion, by letting the *light* into those areas. Whenever pain arises, if I remember to relax completely, I realize it started somewhere in the mind.

Deeply embedded physical memories, like a painful death experience from a past life, can block my mind from God-realization, stopping the harmonic flow and causing physical pain. Early childhood memories as well as past-life memories can be released through yoga practices, meditation, or body therapies.

It is easier to love and forgive everyone (especially myself) when I get into these deeply relaxed states of communion. I have frequently had a pain arise just before a past life memory surfaces for processing.

Our body can lock onto trauma from our lives and hold these tensions, in order to relieve some load from the mind. These stored traumas in our tissues, organs, and bones always have a direct relationship to our mind. Certain healing modalities from the right practitioner can access and release trauma from both past and current lives. Healing can also clear cellular memory patterns (mental, physical, and emotional memories from your parents and ancestors) that manifest unhealthy attitudes and cause disease and pain within our body-mind.

Many modalities of healing are now available, such as direct infusion of light (via mental or physical touch), chiropractic manipulation, structural integration (such as non-force chiropractic), acupressure-meridian therapy, healing with crystals, chakra therapy, massage therapy, and vibrational sound healing. I employ all these in my healing practices. Of course, there are even more modalities of which I am not yet aware.

"FOOD FOR LIGHT" AND CLEANSING

THERE ARE MANY HEALTHY FOOD regimens to lighten and free up our body-mind. I have found the best approach is to eat raw, whole foods, which contain complete enzymes. Consuming whole foods is the most effective way I have found to relax the mind. Whole foods are not only the most nutritional sources to assimilate, but they also have a cooling and alkalizing effect on the body and the digestive tract in particular.

The cooling effect of raw food means that the body works harder to digest it, so raw foodists drop weight naturally on this diet. Losing excess weight effortlessly is a beautiful side effect of the diet. Raw food is rich in enzymes, vitamin, and minerals, which yields the healthiest possible existence and calms our body-mind.

It is much easier to meditate on a raw food diet, and meditation is recommended to allow the living spiritual energy, or *prana*, to enter the body. Clean diets are best complemented by meditation for complete nutrition. I have remained committed to eating only raw foods for at least one month annually. Since 2016, I have been mostly vegan, as I now believe consuming animal products can hold us in a lower vibration. However, I am sure there are exceptions to this rule, as our mind can override anything. I believe that by consuming animal products, we are energetically connected to other people in a field of lower vibratory consciousness, and the animals' blood pollutes our DNA. In order for our body to receive an abundance of *divine light*, it is important to cleanse the body on a regular basis, so light may continue to pour deep into our cellular structure. At the same time, I think it is important to enjoy a variety of foods, as denying one's desire does not work either; although, when we give the body a break, it will cleanse itself.

My favorite experience that proved my body's ability to cleanse occurred during one of my first fasts: a five-day water-and-sunlight fast. Every half hour, I drank a glass of water and went to the bathroom to urinate. By the end of the second day, my urine had started to run clear. On the fourth day, my good friend Don came over, and as I told him how pure I was feeling, he decided to pour perfume on me. He laughed and said, "Now you're not so pure anymore." Though I was annoyed by his thoughtless action, I was amazed how quickly my body ended up excreting the perfume. My next urination was dark yellow, the second and third that followed less so, and by the fourth time I peed, it was absolutely clear again. My body was already in a cleansing mode. Had I not been fasting, I don't know how long this perfume would have been stuck in my body.

I practice a one- to three-day water fast once a year, plus a longer cleanse during another part of the year. During the longer fasts, which focus on cleansing a specific organ of choice and not just the bowels, the body needs nutrients. Taking in nutrients is important for knitting and healing tissues, as opposed to just stripping the toxins out of your cells (which can be accomplished by water fasting). The longest I have fasted is a twelve-day Master Cleanse. This consists purely of lemon, cayenne pepper, maple syrup, and water. This fast cleanses the bowels and bloodstream and is effective at dissolving kidney stones.

Another exemplar fast is the liver and gall bladder cleanse. Although there are many ways to accomplish this fast, I do it intensely: start with seven days of just apple juice (i.e., no solid food, but continue to drink water). One of my early yoga teachers taught me that the malic acid from the apple juice (both fresh and pre-squeezed work fine) softens the stones before they pass. To make sure your bowels are clean, drink two teaspoons of Epsom Salts (magnesium sulfate) dissolved in a quart of warm water on the seventh evening. This mix allows the salty water to match blood density so that the water moves through your digestive tract instead of your renal system (kidneys), cleansing from top to bottom.

DEEP CLEANSING

THE NEXT TWO PARAGRAPHS CONTAIN *explicit descriptions of fasting-related bowel movements. Some readers may wish to skip this section and go to page 102. Additionally, remember that the types of fasts described below should always be supervised by a professional.*

At the age of thirty-three, having fasted annually for thirteen years, on the seventh day of fasting, the Epsom Salts yielded an amazing four full bowel movements within about five hours. The next day, I held down 12 ounces of olive oil mixed with 12 ounces of orange juice. This oil sits in the liver throughout the day and evening, pushing through and out on the ninth morning with the help of a tablespoon of Epsom Salts. (Note: if the oil has already pushed through, skip the second dose of Epsom salt.) On that ninth day, I had another four bowel movements, the final one consisting of the remaining oil with stones floating in it. In total I counted 130 to 150 stones. They ranged from small stones, just a couple of millimeters, all the way up to the size of garbanzo beans. Others on this cleanse have told me they passed stones the size of a quarter dollar. Not everyone produces stones; only 80 percent of the people I put on this fast had them. If you are a stone producer, this fast is recommended every five to ten years. It is my belief that these gallstones are the energy of our calcified anger. When we release them, we also release the anger out of our body. Personally, I have not gotten as angry as I did before completing this fast. But we always get to work on ourselves during this human experience. Always permit your humanity, feelings, and emotions.

After the last bowel movement, I was exhausted and decided to lie down. I had one of the deepest meditative experiences of my life. I could feel my liver breathing as energy coursed through my body. I felt electric blue and gold light flowing through my liver and every cell in my body and mind. It was truly amazing, as I could not tell whether I was awake or asleep in this deep trance. This electric deep state of peace and bliss lasted for well over an hour.

For comprehensive health, our digestive tract is the most important area of cleansing in order to let the *light* in. Spiritual energy is as sunlight entering through our eyes and spreading to every inch of our cells, which then experience that light and begin to vibrate. Our eyes are portals for sunlight. If for any reasons this light is blocked, our body lets us know—first through aches and pains and then inevitably through some type of *dis-ease*. Our body can build up lactic acid in the musculature, plaque in the blood and digestive tract, and stones in the kidneys and gallbladder. Moreover, every curve of our intestines can be filled with undigested matter, which attracts parasites, bacteria, and molds. Getting rid of these poisons slows our aging process. Regular fasting, exercise, and meditation are essential for the sunlight to continue energizing our body-mind. However, please do not attempt any of the aforementioned fasts on your own: it is important to seek professional counsel and supervision.

***

My first guru, Yogananda, told me to fast. At age nineteen, I finished a three-day water fast, and two months later, I drank only water for five days. Not only did I gain self-control, but I also realized I wouldn't die without food. I gained much spiritual insight from fasting, and I began to see people's auras.

Just as the body must cleanse to let more light in, the mind must also clear its personal history. We each have two histories that form our personality: one is our past life history, the complex story of many incarnations; the other is our genetic history, comprised of our DNA, or individual soul lines. The DNA lines hold the thought patterns of our various ethnic origins and diverse cultural belief systems. To clear these beliefs, we must access an accurate memory. It is important to know whether you are remembering what your forbearers believed or whether it is a memory your soul actually holds. Either way, beliefs that separate us and cause fears must be addressed.

Whenever we become aware of a thought, we must ask ourselves, "Is this thought coming from a place of love or from a place of fear?" Illusions come from a place of fear. The entire process of healing comes from, to, and for the mind: when the mind is clear, the heart can finally be accessed more easily. True healing from all unhelpful beliefs comes from a place of love! As we embrace our reality of love, and reject illusions, we grow in our *divine wisdom*.

For example, I have the genetic memories of Abraham, because of the DNA from my father's side. These memories might include intuition for how to raise a child. But this memory did not come from my past lives, though it could have. This genetic memory might give me the intuitive memories of a patriarch, while looking at my own past lives gives me the understanding of gender equality, having been both male and female in different incarnations.

When we look deeply into the mirror of ourselves, we eventually can see a clear reflection of God. Then we may ask, "What do I truly desire?" Our deepest desire is always in perfect alignment with *divine will.* Never settle for what does not feel one hundred percent right. Never forget your wholeness or your holiness. Embrace God's presence, and banish your fear reactions. Release them down to the smallest details of your life, knowing that today's needs will be met, no matter where you might be at the time. Of course I cannot give you this; you must build your own relationship with God and experience that trust.

During my own journey, negative energies have frequently approached me and endangered my consciousness with feelings of insecurity and negative self-image. Once we become awakened *beings of light,* we can perceive and participate in the spiritual creation more fully, seeing the good and evil in the world around us. Thus, becoming aware of both energies, dark and light, we must develop an effective system of self-protection—a kind of spiritual armor. Denial of negativity is the only proper use of denial. The dark side will test you, offering power and wealth, if fear fails to persuade you.

As an example, during the first year of awakening, as my love grew, I trusted more and more in the moment's perfection. During a very deep meditation, a large green dragon appeared before me. The dragon sat on a throne and looked scary to me. The creature stretched out its hand and with telepathy told me that if I kissed its hand, I could have all the power and wealth in the world. There was no hesitation or debate for me. I asked it to go away and continued to praise God (as an aside, later in life, I realized there are also good dragons).

The darkness cannot threaten us, as spirit is truly alive in both the dark and light—the dark being our teacher and allowing free will. When we evolve into our full potential of cosmic consciousness, we realize God's will and human will exist as two aspects of one reality. The Holy Spirit always wishes for us to grow while possessing free will, to make choices for ourselves. Dark and light energy work together, and having a body can teach this to us. The body that has been placed in duality is the teacher for our *eternal soul*. No matter what you've done in life—good or bad—we will always exist within our *original innocence*, as your soul cannot change.

Even once we have recognized our connection to God, we might still want to be separate, or believe we are separate, and choose to live apart from God. Even the most focused souls can get lost in a moment or a lifetime of fear, when we live in the material world. When we sense the loss of our spiritual connection, in order to fill the void, we may turn toward alcohol, mind-altering drugs, the pursuit of money, or worst of all: television.

Before I gave the Casa Linda motel back to my parents, I had to completely stop watching television. An experience I had while watching a Duran Duran music video in the mid-1980s freaked me out! A red devil ran across my screen, paused to look at me, and then kept running. I believed I must have seen a subliminal image, so I waited for the show to air again eight hours later. When the video came on again and the image was not there, I did not just turn the TV off; I pulled the cable out of the wall! I did not want to be subliminally influenced by watching TV.

To my dismay, this red devil image I saw gained popularity over the years. I later found this exact devil image in tattoo books, and again saw it on slot machines in different casinos I visited while staying with my parents after they moved to Las Vegas, Nevada. It has been many years since I overcame my television addiction, although I do enjoy going to the movie theater occasionally. I thank God for giving me the strength to stop the things that truly don't serve my highest good.

Nowadays, I notice people are also surfing the internet and getting lost.

Transcending the constant use of alcohol, drugs, television, and social media is a first step on the divine spiritual path, as our mind must eventually become present in every moment. Changing how we eat is also a vital step in our conscious *light-body evolution*. The light-body has the ability to touch, smell, speak, and see. The extent to which you have developed these faculties in your physical body influences the sensory capacity your light body will have once your body has burned away.

Our diets affect our body's ability to hold light; even after three days of just fruits and vegetables, my body relaxes and my chakras open. It is crucial to get away from fast foods, deep-fried foods, processed foods, soda, and sugar. Consuming less meat is also recommended for most A and B blood types, but some O types benefit from some meat. I do recommend a diet high in protein. To stay grounded, I eat lots of nuts, avocados, and greens, which are very high in protein. For the O blood type, I also would recommend organic eggs and wild-caught fish. The human body needs time—sometimes years—to change a diet without going into shock. Allow this process of changing your diet to start feeding your light body to take time.

In the Essene Gospels, found in the Dead Sea Scrolls, Jesus exhorts us to let in the Mother Earth's angels: Sunlight, Air, and Water. Christ suggests in these writings that when we first cleanse the body and it has been purified by the Mother Earth's angels, only then can we learn directly from the Father's angels in the hierarchies of light, from the cherubim to the seraphim. There are many books on angels (see *Watch Your Dreams* in "Suggested Further Reading" in the appendix). Our body-minds are directly affected by the foods we consume. Simply stated: eat whole raw foods. Eventually, work up to 70 or 90 percent whole foods. God already prepared our food to perfection on trees and vines. There are, of course, some foods (e.g., rice, potatoes) that gain nutrition after being combusted by cooking. We cannot make our bodies, and specifically our blood, any cleaner than when we are on this pure raw and whole food diet, versus any other diet I have found. Also, karma-free eating (eating strictly vegetarian) helps us to let go of stuck emotional patterns—avoiding the fear energies the animal kingdoms hold and releasing those energies from our emotional body.

Beyond a change of eating habits, we must let go of all fears and worries. We each must come to our own level of trust in God. The more faith we have, the more we can trust in a good outcome from any situation. Even without faith, this type of trust can develop by having been raised by a loving family. The extent to which you have trust or faith determines how much spirit can give in return. To release our karma in the world, we can earn a living in ways that provide others with something meaningful. Do things you are passionate about. I am passionate about doing body therapies for others, and in doing so, I have earned my income by helping relieve others' bodies and minds from pain. Your inner reality creates your outer experience; your heart, not your words, manifests your reality.

Spend your free time well. I drum, dance, write, and play all types of games with others. Officiating wedding ceremonies and, of course, practicing and teaching yoga make me happy. Be creative, and by all means, nurture all your relationships, whether it is a stranger that passes you or your best lifelong friend.

A VISITATION

AT SOME POINT, BE IT the present incarnation or in the future, everyone must go inside and examine their own darkness before they can really see the light and play well with others. Ingesting hallucinogens helped me to investigate myself and raise my energy levels. With the help of hallucinogens, I have developed a longer attention span, occasionally achieving pure hearing and seeing (i.e., from the Holy Spirit), which has helped to clear out my own misperceptions. Nevertheless, it is important to come back out of the hallucinogen-induced inner journey. Mind-altering substances never kept me in a great state of mind or feeling for a prolonged period. They did, however, give me insights into spiritual living. Only my love for God—and not mind-altering substances—kept me on the higher planes, from where we can see the movement of spirit and in a place of self-love, where consciousness endured.

Throughout my life, none of my spiritual masters ever made themselves known to me while I was on hallucinogens. I have received much spiritual help, but it seems I have only seen divine beings when sober, aside from one time.

One of the spiritual teachers who interact with me frequently is the ascended master Saint Germaine, a French Christian saint, known as the keeper of the *violet ray of light*. He began to work with me early on, during my mid-twenties. I'd see his face from time to time, or I'd simply perceive a violet energy field when he was present—especially while I was doing energy healing work. On one such occasion, I had eaten a tiny dose—maybe half a gram—of hallucinogenic mushrooms at a Grateful Dead show. Of course, I went into a long prayer to start my journey. The show began about thirty minutes later, just as I started to perceive the *higher mind*: I was gaining awareness of thoughts that created reality. I was understanding my connection to others' minds and my responsibility to hold peace for them. I immediately noticed that the music was struggling a bit, and as I observed the band, I perceived that two band members on guitar and keyboard were in some sort of psychic argument. I looked at Jerry Garcia; he was trying to ignore the disharmony and remain focused on his guitar. I was bummed to have gotten high and then have to observe the psychic disharmony within the band.

I began to pray for some sort of intervention to re-harmonize the band, because I did not want to hear it. Within half a minute of praying, I observed a violet field of energy above the stage. Seeing the field of light, I also noticed a violet flame off to the right of the stage. To my surprise, Saint Germaine stood under the flame— approximately twenty feet tall! Instantaneously, he shot his right arm forward at the band, the violet light filled the stage, and the music immediately caught fire! So much light came through that nobody could think at all. The music took off, and everyone began dancing hard. As I boogied the night away, I gave thanks for the vision and for my answered prayer.

Experiencing and practicing love for God brings us to a place where all of creation may bow to that love within us. When we take everyone into an embrace of divine love within ourselves, we are possessed by the immense power of love. We can manifest the spiritual power to help clear the stuck thoughts of everyone around us so they may enjoy the present moment. This good work then keeps our own self clear and eventually helps to clear everyone in this world. Until we reach complete and enduring clarity within a drug-free, unaltered state of mind, we will struggle to maintain our focus on our loving God. Unless someone already has schizophrenia or a family history of anything that resembles the disorder, I could not recommend trying mushrooms, ayahuasca, and marijuana, which are medicines from the Mother Earth prepared for our growth. However, if one does try these substances, they should be used under the direction of a spiritual guide to provide brief assistance in one's spiritual growth process. Importantly, please stay away from pills, powders, or continuous use of any substance!

ON HELPING

MY GURU, YOGANANDA, SUGGESTS THAT a truly enlightened person can help sustain the focus of a hundred or more people and that when more enlightened beings come together, the numbers multiply. A truly awakened being may help heal and bring those around them into bliss, as long as people are willing. We can never claim that we are God or be equal to God, but we can be at one with God.

The universe will always let us do what we want with our time and energies. Free will is a choice we have within our circumstances on earth. It is our response to our particular circumstances: *I AM choosing to stay in harmony no matter what the outer reality is doing* (though, of course, I still might occasionally lose my presence of mind and flip someone off while driving). In my experience, staying in harmony helps me to realize a state of being that is *for* love and not *against* anything. Staying in harmony allows me to be more focused. Concentrating on the *eternal* state of my being, my life flows, as I know spirit is creating perfection on my behalf. Hopefully, this state of flow then becomes our effortless, childlike nature.

Now, I find I can help most by being my most authentic self, plugging up holes in the *etheric fabric* (the subtle field of energy that holds creation together). The holes are caused by the fears and projections of others around me. The *mass mind-and-heart spaces* of our chakras form a place where wholeness and non-separation can be felt. A slight vigilant awareness of these mind-and-heart spaces allows me to avoid taking on the negative patterns of others as light fills in these holes.

I believe we need many more people doing this type of spiritual work, which is at its core just the practice of instant forgiveness. I do love everyone as myself, but maybe I do not like them, as they don't like themselves yet. Forgiving people is really loving them even when you're repulsed. Love is always *for-giving*! I had never realized before my spiritual awakening how much we are all a part of each other. There is one energy field and one thought field, but if you're not interacting with everyone positively and ruling your mind, you are subjected to the ups and downs of others.

It is so important not to let any thoughts slip by unconsciously: your own thoughts or anybody else's. Thoughts must be accompanied by feelings; thinking without feeling leaves us cold, and we can lose the trust and faith that all things are being guided in perfection. It is much less effective for God to be helping you if you are unaware of it. Just a single moment of unawareness can allow us to slip back into worry, fear, anger, grief, or overexertion. When you're in a state of feeling and not thought, this process of trusting in the perfection becomes much easier.

Once again, we are never going to be equal to God, but we can always remember to be in the oneness and wholeness that we truly are! Everything is actually made of light; we only think of ourselves as separate. Fears cause judgments, separating people and religious organizations. We really should just be working on ourselves! That is what helps everyone around us the most.

Some of the unique experiences I have had certainly overwhelmed me—like the first time I consciously left my body or when I first saw Christ. I have tried and succeeded to knock myself out of consciousness many times, forgetting the *higher mind*. We can be shut down easily, by things like smoking too much marijuana, eating too much, or obsessing on any thought, such as something we lack or lost love. Throughout my moments of lower consciousness in this incarnation, my guides have continued to show up for me to remind me of spiritual commitments and to not let me off the proverbial hook. As I age and gain wisdom, it becomes easier to face my destiny. We take responsibility for our own thought projections, yet we entrust the outcome to God.

In the beginning of mankind, many eons ago, reincarnation did not exist; there was no need for it. Luckily, God loves us so much that *spirit* began to recycle souls. Now, instead of being punished for our actions, we get to try again and again, always as God's self (in male or female form). Our energy cannot be destroyed, anyway: it just changes form. In addition to God, the wonderful deified beings, ascended masters and other gurus of this plane, all keep reminding me that I am not alone in this life experience. I also owe so much gratitude to friends, angels, and the Mother Earth's own conscious awareness, in addition to the earth's higher conscious beings.

I am writing this book not to gratify myself but to share with all beings that are awakening now—to encourage their faith, growth, and wholeness. I wish to help people get beyond the dogmatic structures that have kept us asleep or in the unconscious collective. I write this to stop the negative intentions of beings that want to control or stop God's love from entering into the creation. Love is the highest frequency of consciousness and must bloom in everyone's heart on earth, as it is being expressed in heaven.

It is foolish to buy into fear or insecurity of any kind—about food or shelter, for example. All these fears are separation from your own mind, instead of having a basic confidence and trusting the perfection. As I take responsibility for my thoughts and feel wholeness, my every need is met. We need to test this for ourselves and build our own relationship with the universe, as I cannot give this to anyone. Internal reality creates the outer experience, allowing reality to manifest more easily.

Experiencing and practicing love for God in a pointed focus brings us to a place where all creation may bow to the love for God within us. When we take everyone into an embrace of divine love, seeing past their problems, we stand in wholeness. Then love possesses the *spiritual power* to awaken everyone in the world to divine love itself, one soul at a time.

Until we reach complete and enduring clarity within a drug-free and unaltered state of mind, not split by stupefying media or bad relationships, the struggle to keep our body-mind whole continues. Anyone with sincere desire can gather with spiritual people, which helps bring us all into a state of spiritual awareness and bliss. This is exemplified in positive environments such as churches, nature, as well as at concerts, where many people feel uplifted.

Simply by holding yourself together, you will be filling the *mass mind-and-heart spaces* with light. I believe we need many more people doing this kind of work. Even if people call you lazy or spaced out, please continue to hold focus. *The world will never see a spiritual person as having accomplished enough.*

The ego or mind cannot get it; only the heart can understand *spirit* and feel your connection to the omnipresence, actualizing the truth. The true meditative state is one of receptivity: free from thought. I love everyone as I love myself, even if they cannot yet receive that love. I choose to feel good. Feeling is believing; it is like a huge holographic field of light, energy, and thought, which we reprogram every time we meditate.

Thoughts are things that have weight. In order to hold light, it is so important not to let negative thoughts come through your brain unconsciously—your own thoughts or, if you are sensitive, anyone else's.

Everything is made of light; we only *think* ourselves into a state of separation, and the world supports that view. When we spend too much time in our different religious orientations, the darkness will use that to separate us from each other. Don't all religions say to love? We must let everyone actually get to work on themselves while experiencing free will! This is important. Even if they don't choose the *light,* this choice must be respected.

Saint Germaine warns us not to get stuck in the psychic realms and not to get stuck in debate with other beings or disembodied entities, lost souls who are stuck on this plane but outside of our visual range. I have witnessed these beings in bars, vicariously drinking and smoking through people and influencing them. Remember the Creator and stay with the feeling of peace. Live in heart-centered awareness, even if you're seeing other planes of existence.

It is nice to have the help and be reminded of our spiritual commitments. As I gain in years, the destiny of my truth becomes more present so that it gets easier simply to let go and live.

This body is our vehicle, but we are not just this body: we are simply in it while gaining responsibility for our creations.

I write to stop the negative intentions of beings that have manipulated reality, those who want to control or stop God from entering into the creation—either consciously or, like corporations, unconsciously. This planet has been fear-based for too long. I mean, how much money is enough?

Mankind, out of fear, has been in a perpetual state of war on this planet. It is insane to continue buying into this fear program or into any kind of fear. The more I focus internally, the more easily the outer reality manifests for me. Through all the negative influences, I continue to pray for others.

With time, as soon as that first fear or worry creeps in, your energy levels drop. With fear closing the upper chakras, the state of awareness diminishes, semi-lost until the next meditation or super conscious event (like a good concert or church service) that would lift the spirit. For me, it seems more and more that daily meditation is essential—sometimes more than once a day—to maintain awareness. It doesn't matter how much time you spend in the stillness of meditation, whether it is just five minutes or five hours, as long as you reestablish the feeling of contact with the Creator.

The Muslim religion has two sects: Shiite and Sunni. Sunni followers suggest making contact three times per day, while the other suggests five times. Yogananda suggests that we should sit in meditation each morning and night, resisting sleep while doing so, in addition to a multiple hour-long deep meditation once per week. He claimed that meditation speeds up our evolution more than prayer does.

The interesting thing about the chakra system is that one may easily see down into the lower centers from the upper chakras; however, one cannot necessarily see into the upper center from the bottom ones, until they are opened through practice or by grace. When you open the upper chakras again, the memories of the *higher self* reconnect, from all the previous times you were in that in that higher state.

I will describe the Hindu terms regarding consciousness: First, there is the state of Samadhi, the God-enlightened state of bliss, which is still in flux. Then, in Nirvikalpa Samadhi, the final state of union with God while in a body, you no longer leave the state of deep peace. This process culminates in the Mahasamadhi, which is the final conscious exit from the body and had been the highest state of evolution in Hinduism. When Christ came, he opened up the possibility of human *ascension* by ascending himself and setting the pattern into the field of light in this realm. Through ascension, you can take your body with you by shifting the cellular structure via an accelerated state of vibration. The body's cells increase in heat and vibrational intensity proportional to the amount of light coming down on you. With the ultimate level of ascension, our frequency shifts, heating us to over 2,000 degrees Fahrenheit, effectively burning off the outer shell (the body). This leaves behind a little golden-white ash (proven by the Shroud of Turin, upon which Christ's visage was burned at the location of his face at his moment of ascension).

Once we have gone through many levels of change, we are transfigured into the light body, which maintains the abilities to smell, taste, touch, hear, and see. As the light body develops, we gain these pre-ascension skills that have to be developed at the physical level before ascension becomes possible. It is quite possible that many human beings have ascended since the time of the Lord Christ. The ascended masters choose either to stay on this plane to help here or to leave here and go to another planet where souls might be more evolved.

Wherever you look, the light goes, and wherever the light goes, healing begins to happen. If you are seeing darkness, the light will begin to dissolve it, as long as you keep gazing there without fears. We are at one with God! The goal always is to get rid of the blocks that stop us from seeing that oneness. Should darkness persist without seeming to move, then ask for help. The *ascended beings*, or angels, will always answer a sincere request.

Even though so many *higher beings* have approached me and I love them all dearly, I feel especially close to Jesus. He feels like my older brother and interacts with me a couple times a year (at least that I am aware of). He is always subtle and never directly tells me to do anything; instead, he makes suggestions, like any good teacher.

We often have no contact with the ascended masters for long periods, as we need to establish our own contact with God. As we get quiet, we can always come into our own *higher presence*, humbly feeling the state of God awareness as ourselves.

Everyone must release their own suffering before the angelic kingdoms may intervene; they will not interfere with your karma. Only God can do that, and he will not interfere except to receive your love. Love is irresistible to God. God, our heavenly *mother-father*, needs our love, just as we need God's love; thusly is the spiritual marriage completed. When this marriage occurs, we are exempted from laws of this world's karma. At that point, we are translocated into the kingdom of light, moving up from the third dimension and hearing the angels, which is one of the first true steps toward gaining a spiritual consciousness versus a religious awareness. There are many steps thereafter before our final ascension into *light*.

When Christ took the keys of death from the world after being the first to ascend, the dark force, angered at the possible loss of control, inhabited the very next soul to incarnate. This initiated the process whereby all candidates for ascension would also be inhabited by the darkness of the world, and then made to overcome it, thus bringing love, light, and healing to this beautiful life-giving planet. This first of these oppressed souls, through many incarnations, eventually became the ascended master Saint Germaine—keeper of the violet flame of ascension, which is the base chakra's red light merging through the blue throat chakra to create violet in the crown chakra.

God did not wish to create robots, which is why everything here on earth is allowed, including the ability to love and step into our eternal consciousness. It is our spiritual inheritance and everybody's birthright. The desire for power and wealth comes from the reptilian part of our brain, just as the desire for peace and love comes from the parts unique to mammalian beings. When we realize we have the choice to practice love and forgiveness and we are truly cared for by the universe, only then will true power be ours to wield. Prosperity is part of our natural spiritual awakening: it is one of the gifts given by Christ's perfect example of the human-and-spirit union.

GRATEFUL DEAD CONCERTS

AS I HAVE TRAVELED THE world, I have also attended many Grateful Dead concerts. So many of the people at these shows were alive in the spirit of the *divine*: colorful people dancing their way up the spiritual ladder. The (Grateful) Dead gave me a sense of belonging, a deep feeling of being home in a judgment-free environment. People who are focused on the same thing can easily create a one-mind experience, and music is one of the greatest doorways to spiritual awareness. By listening and staying in time with the music, you can stay in the moment of creation.

Soon after my spiritual awakening, I realized it was not just me this was happening to—what a relief! Many people were awakening spiritually, and more and more people were seeing their true omnipresent nature and experiencing visions of the divine light. I came to realize people all around the world were gradually realizing their interconnected natures and were beginning to live their lives more grounded in love and trust. I noticed the people around me were coming to perceive that we share one heart and one mind, creating a true sense of family.

There were many times in my early twenties (and rarely, this still happens today) that I fell back into the world of the ego, feeling separate from everything and alone. That was when I would really struggle. It was easy to worry that I was doing the wrong thing, instead of trusting my own true light nature. Many of my old friends and my blood-related family did not understand my new perspective. To them, my not wanting to find a job or become a lawyer was shocking. I was so blissed out. Nobody understood that I loved them unconditionally, being in this no-mind state of awareness. Most people thought I was hitting on them or gay or that I had some type of ulterior motive simply because I was smiling so much. During this time, many people were afraid to receive my love. When love is received, it creates more love; when not received, it can create fear. To anything that is not light, light burns!

My Tao (path) of choosing between the world of light and the world of darkness began in my early twenties, and continues to be a constant choice. Much later in life I realized it was much easier to stay spiritually conscious around my spiritually awakened "family"; thus, I have spent time cultivating these relationships.

The (Christian) Holy Bible's Book of Revelation suggests there would be two minds in the future: One is the mind of the *beast*, which I realized is the military industrial complex and corporations. The other mind is composed of the people who would work toward the good of the whole and are selflessly helping, even if by just holding the light, staying focused on being loving.

We begin to see God, in the light and in the dark, doing a dance. God allows free will so we can learn from our mistakes to help our souls and the world to evolve. It seems that in every galactic time cycle, man makes bad choices out of fear. However, this time, in my belief, God will not allow us to destroy ourselves again, as we may have done in other periods, other civilizations, and even other planets.

The Grateful Dead concerts I attended helped me to become the child who used to think he was an adult. The return to innocence is our goal as spiritual beings. Many people came to realize their own childlike God-self at these concerts, having realized that our oneness and childlike nature allow us to renounce all worldly, corporate, antisocial, and industrial structures. I felt deeply that a new world of *love* was coming, and I feel this even more strongly now. It was at this time in my life that I began to walk in two different worlds: the world of man and the mundane and the world of God and magic.

As this split in consciousness in myself and others became more evident, I also realized that God, as love, would have a place elsewhere on another planet for those who would choose a third dimensional reality, as the Earth herself was to be lifted to a higher frequency. Realizing my need to love all, I began honoring all people who would choose that third dimensional reality, including its warlike and fear-based awareness. Finally understanding and honoring that everyone's reality is truly their expression of free will gave me a lot more peace.

The Dead shows allowed for love. With people watching your thoughts, it becomes easier to be aware of your actions and intentions, which helps to further love. Many people experienced psychic healing during these concerts. Their healing, as well as my healing, was the blessing of collective consciousness, the blessing of observing God in action—something I had not been privy to as a child within my family dynamic. Of course, many people there who were on drugs and alcohol obviously got lost at these shows and got stuck in different astral planes—places of consciousness beyond the third dimension where whatever you dream of manifests to the senses. Getting stuck in the astral plane, one cannot witness the surrender of the soul to the *universal mind* and never access the heavenly *etheric planes* beyond the *astral*.[1] For me, heart and mind came together in God's presence at Dead concerts, deep within the divine silence.

I was once gifted with 360-degree vision during a very powerful Dead show, which lasted for a few hours and left me in awe. The clarity, power, and peace that arose were overwhelming, but I greatly enjoyed the experience. When it was over, I walked out of the arena, elated and blissed out. In a state of complete thankfulness, I decided I now needed a *guru* to give me a spiritual name. I heard a quiet, powerful voice tell me, "Give yourself a name," and immediately the name rolled out of my consciousness: Arjuna Vishnu Ananda Das.

After this momentous occasion of receiving my spiritual name, I returned to Lake Tahoe and quit the motel business; in fact, I completely quit the world for a while. I had seen that people were dropping out of society, disenchanted with the status quo. Many were headed toward a higher vision of what life could be if they were devoted to God, living as love in the present moment. I wanted to join the higher mind of collective consciousness and lose my fear of

---

[1] By *grace*, I didn't get stuck in the delusion or power of the *astral plane*. One friend of mine who did could leave his body and dream anything he wanted from there: girls, food, whatever. He was stuck there for years doing heroin.

survival. Choosing to not work or study scared my parents; they did not understand my changes in behavior at all.

Even though I felt a new dependence on spirit, I retained five thousand dollars that I had certainly earned. I gave the motel and my sports car back to my parents; I surrendered everything I had owned. I bought a used white 1972 VW bus for two thousand five hundred dollars: my new home for the next couple of years. I gave away much of the remaining half slowly, buying a ticket for someone else at every show I went to until I ran out of money.

I was not just following the Grateful Dead; I couldn't follow a one-dimensional path such as being a Dead Head. It seemed to me that some people had gotten lost in the hippy lifestyle. I really wanted to learn everything, and to understand God everywhere, so I visited temples and churches along the way. I would camp and talk with people everywhere—wealthy or poor, lost or found, functional or dysfunctional. I really wanted to know how people got to where they were in their lives. I found many people were living out of society by choice. I realized that God existed beyond anybody or anything. That deep realization continues to be my experience. I cannot just join one organization of any kind or just one expression of God's love. I find many to attend.

***

One experience especially stands out. I had not gotten a ticket to get into the show at the Oakland Coliseum in Northern California, so instead, I walked over to a drum circle that was happening near the entrance. I was still just twenty-one years old, and with all the spiritual insights I was having, I felt psychically empowered. There were maybe a hundred or more people drumming and dancing around who also had not gotten into the show. I began to focus on my third eye, thinking to myself, *I am going to use my imagination and force of will to expand the energy and love of this gathering.* I had just begun to focus when I heard a small voice saying, "Oh, really? Watch this." My being was instantly immobilized. All my attention went to my forehead. I felt a knot of pressure form in between my eyebrows, and it started moving upwards. Immediately, the volume, energy, and excitement of the group increased. I briefly opened my eyes to see the drummers being lifted into their spiritual bodies and their third eyes opening. The pressure of the knot increased and rose slowly toward my hairline, with the volume of the drums increasing and expanding in tandem. Everyone began singing and cheering. Looking deep into the knot, the pressure still increasing in my forehead, I began to see a beautiful blue light; a deep sky blue filled my vision and created a tunnel. My mind flew down the tunnel, and I was enveloped by a deep peace. Suddenly, I was redirected back into my body, but above my head, energy was moving and opening my vision even more. My vision opened slowly in a circular fashion, beginning at my forehead and going to my right. I was then able to see behind my head and all the way around the left side. The blue light was everywhere. I felt spirits flying around me saying, "You are in the body of Christ." As they repeated those words, I also had a sense of 360-degree vision.

Right then an anonymous person in the crowd yelled out, "Arjuna!" I accepted this was the spiritual name I had given myself, but I worried about this name being my *ego*. Worry is the same as fear, and as fear entered, the vision stopped, the experienced ended, and I was overwhelmed with confusion. I walked away from the circle dazed, thinking about what had just happened. I couldn't get my vision back up to the spiritual eye, as I was worrying about doing the wrong thing in life. I wandered around, discombobulated, for about fifteen minutes. I eventually noticed energetic colors flying around a teepee that was a couple hundred yards away, and I walked over. As I neared the teepee, I heard people chanting, "Hare Krishna." I was really unsure about these people, but the energy attracted me (keep in mind, I was still absolutely sober). Hesitantly, I sat in the doorway instead of going all the way in, where there were six people chanting. As I closed my eyes and began to pray along, I was once again blown away. I could see everyone in the teepee even with my eyes closed. As the main swami sat erect with his chest thrust out, a green light first pushed through this man's chest, and then through everyone's chest, including mine. It physically moved me. The green light from everyone's chest came together in the center of the teepee and swirled upward and out through the opening at the top. My mind moved with the light, and I saw an infinite expanse of space and stars. As soon as the light ascended, I heard a million beings chanting, "Hare Krishna," the *universal choir of praise*. It was so beautiful. I don't know how long I listened in total, and I never talked to any of the men in the teepee.

For weeks after that experience, I continued to hear the choir anytime I closed my eyes. A month later, I was back in my parents' home in Lake Tahoe for a visit, fear crept in suddenly when I realized the words of a verse in the Hare Krishna chant, "Hare Rama," sound like the name of Nazi general Erwin Rommel (in German: "Herr Rommel"). My fear of serving the dark side in any way silenced the choir, sadly, and I did not hear it again. In retrospect, I see that was a superbly dumb fear, but I was young, and I did not know all my past life history yet. Namely, I did not yet know about my connection to the benevolent Blue Race or about my life as a rabbi in Auschwitz, which changed many of my present perceptions. Had I known about my past lives then, I certainly would not have gone into fear in that situation.

***

At another Grateful Dead show a few months later at the Kaiser Convention Center, also in Oakland, I experienced a fall from grace. A small dose of magic mushrooms led me to an energized yet relaxed state of mind, and I sat close to the stage with a couple people I had not met but with whom I immediately got along well. They pulled out a marijuana joint, and I was soon feeling really good.

The show began and the music permeated my being. Everyone began to dance. By the second song the whole auditorium was dancing happily. Well beyond thought, I was boogying away, when I noticed a guy was standing still in front of me. I had the thought, *I wish this guy would move.* Jerry Garcia gave me a dirty look and changed the song midway through. The man immediately began to dance. I felt as if the universe had heard my negative thought and I had disturbed the silent unity. Then I noticed that Bobby Weir, another band member, had taken over leading the music. I realized this was due to my interference in the thought field, and I was suddenly aware of my unity with all beings.

Bobby's face started changing in front of me; he looked like a ghoul. My mind reeled as the negative vision interfered with my dancing. I looked down and saw a black void coming up from the bottom of my feet. I immediately began to say a "Hail, Mary" prayer. But it was too late: the black void enveloped my body, and I passed out. As I slowly came to, sitting on my butt in a smoke-filled crowd, it was now dark out. Some time must have passed; I had no idea how much. I heard a voice saying, "Do you want me to take you to the hospital?" I looked around in a daze, and with the smoke and dancing colorful legs everywhere, my first thought was, *I must be in hell.* Now, I realize it was all my false perception. I heard the voice again: "Do you want me to take you to the hospital?" This time, I realized he was talking to me. I shook it off and told him no. He helped me up and walked me to the bathroom. He helped me selflessly even though we did not know each other. After I washed up, I looked at him. He was tall, was slightly heavyset, and had long red hair. At first, I pulled back from him.

Because of some intrusive past life consciousness, my first thought was that of judgment, and this negative thought interfered with my vision. However, this time I caught myself and thought: *What an asshole I am. This guy just helped me.* I thanked him for helping me pull it back together.

The belief that I was in hell still plagued me, but I overcame it and slowly rejoined the show from the back of the theater. I did not know then that I had been holding judgment, but I released my leftover judgments of people that day—especially of red-haired people.[2]

As I pulled it back together after my perceived fall from consciousness, I was glad that God had revealed to me this judgmental part of my ego, which was certainly not going to be serving the planet or myself any longer.

The heart energy must emerge on earth now. When judgment stops on the planet, love can catch up to our technological advances so we do not destroy this planet. In my own spiritual timeline, with God's grace, it was only when I was completely out of judgment that I saw people's wholeness, and I became able to give and receive love a little more.

---

[2] Later, in deep contemplation, I remembered that the Egyptians had fought with a red-haired race in one of my past lives. I assume this is why I had held this prejudice. A couple of years later, I even noticed some red-haired people were naturally carrying the violet ray frequency, or *violet flame*. Of course, everyone can integrate with it; the red base chakra moves up through the blue throat chakra and creates the *violet crown*. As all people start integrating the different frequencies held by different races—via mixed racial birth or activating ourselves through meditation—we will be able to understand each other more easily as people. I realized that the less I judged, the more I saw. I was so happy to have integrated with the violet ray—by the grace of Saint Germaine—during Reiki initiations.

POLARITY OF FREQUENCY

NOTICING MY OWN MIND BEING in a state of confusion between negative and positive realities of our existence, I slowly learned not to pay too much attention to the outer reality, depending instead on the truth inside myself—focusing on the inner heaven. We are cocreators with the divine, and our inner harmony creates our outer reality. We magnetize our desires into our lives, whether it is wealth, power, or peace of mind.

What has often stopped me from having comfort and peace was mistrust of the government or of corporate financial powers that influence the news we watch or of those who valued personal gain over human life. There are even alien and other dimensional influences, which spread fear, consciously or out of ignorance, to divide and conquer, lowering our collective frequencies of light. Despite all this negativity, I've found that the more I take responsibility for my inner reality, the more I trust in spirit, letting go of the outcome yet praying for the light.

I now understand that people are experiencing their karma individually or collectively. People incarnate into the situation they have earned or desired either in past lives or in the current life. People may incarnate in states of fear and disharmony or in states of peace.

As I realized I could overcome my negative karma, I also realized people must let go of their own fear-based realities to allow in the flow of light, all in their own time. I find that a collective shift of consciousness is possible, at least for a group of souls if not for all. I find that we are in a *war for frequency*. Let's define frequency as the rate at which your mind and cells vibrate. The love frequency has a different vibration than that of fear. I find it validating to believe that there is a conscious intention to keep people at higher frequencies from gaining their inner power; *the powers that be* fear losing control. I am also comforted to know the light is coming to this planet. Separating people by religion, skin color, monetary status, sexual orientation, and other forms of identity gives control to the powers that be by keeping people in a state of worry or fear.

We must empower ourselves by letting go of F.E.A.R. (false evidence appearing real). Realizing that I am not alone and have support from other planes of light helps me become more and more fearless as I release the split in my consciousness (the split between being lost on earth or being an omnipresent living soul). We heal more and more as the light gets stronger on the earth.

Remember: as the light gets stronger, the darkness can seem stronger. But know that this happens only because when the light shines, the darkness becomes more apparent.

PAST-LIFE KARMA

THE FIRST PAST LIFE VISIONS I had while on Dead tour were as a priest in the Ancient Egyptian monarchy, and those Egyptian memories took a couple of years to energetically clear. I had another in Germany during World War II as a rabbi imprisoned in a concentration camp—both not super-fun memories.

During an American Indian pipe ceremony, I smoked one drag of a tobacco pipe (although I do not condone the use of tobacco). After the leader of the ceremony led some long prayers, and only moments after exhaling the smoke, my mind quieted. I visually saw myself in at least twenty different incarnations. Each face flashed by me for about one second—mostly males but some females—with different garbs and from many historical periods. All the incarnations seemed simple to me, like Stone Age hunter-gatherers, fishermen, and farmers. I realized later that these memories were all from insignificant lives where no major karma had been incurred. After they flashed by, for about an hour, I did not know what I looked like in my current life stream.

My guru, Deva Yogananda, suggested we should not look for our past lives; instead, what is important is *this* life and working toward the next incarnation or liberation from this world. However, if positive or negative karma from past lives reveals itself, we should embrace it lovingly to remove any negative influences on our current incarnation.

Past lives that have not yet been cleared can cause negative personality traits to surface in the present life. In particular, this happens in interpersonal relationships, where I react to certain people in a negative way before I can understand why. So, as these lives have come up for me, I've investigated the past incarnations and cleared these personality flaws that hamper my life, clearing anything that is no longer serving me. Very few lives I have seen were empowering—mostly, I saw my flaws. Also, because on some level, all lives are coexisting, through meditation practice and loving forgiveness of *self* and others, our past, our present, and hopefully our future can be harmonized in our current life. Only in *this* moment can all things be harmonized.

I was playing music with my friend, Fast Eddie, with whom I had performed a few duo gigs together over the years. Eddie had asked me to join him for a Halloween jam. He played guitar and harmonica, and I joined him on hand drums. We played well together, and I was enjoying myself. Although I was deeply involved in the music, my attention continued to drift toward a psychic reader. She had set up shop in the corner of the bar. She was charging forty dollars for a reading.

During the break in the set, I was magnetized to her. I pulled my last twelve dollars out of my pocket and offered it to her. She asked me to sit down. Partway through the reading, she asked me if I remembered my time walking with Christ, and if I remembered who I was. I said I did not. Nor did I remember that incarnation, but I did notice my strong affinity for Jesus, even though I was not raised Christian. After telling her that, she told me I was on the verge of remembering a very powerful lifetime. I thought about this reading for weeks, wondering what she could have meant—before all the memories hit me.

Joel, my wonderful Reiki teacher, gave me a generous amount of body therapy, including deep-tissue massage and energy work. He would do such deep massage with the energy healing that at times, it was painful. We both understood that physical pain in the body was resistance to the divine within us, so I relaxed through the physical blockages as much as possible to release its karma.

All through my young adulthood, and even after much spiritual healing, I carried shoulder and back pain. At different times, the release of this pain would lead to Joel or me having visions in relationship to the pain. These visions could reveal old wounds from knives, swords, or spears stuck in the etheric body. Memories come up when they're ready to be healed and released. These remembrances will happen naturally.

Everyone has the potential to heal every aspect of themselves without remembering past lives, but remembering can give us more tools to work with. After all, how can we heal if we do not understand the different aspects of ourselves?

Past-life memories can only unfold from already knowing and trusting in divine perfection. Without trusting, these traumas might recur in our current body-minds. All healing must first happen in the mind. We can release anything if we can become detached from the outcome of past karmic visions.

On the other hand, so much karma can be cleared with loving parents in the first five years of life—if conscious, loving parents are involved and paying attention. In addition, anything can be healed— even without the karma of conscious and loving parents, even without the concept of healing ever coming to conscious awareness.

***

The psychic's promise came true, three weeks after her reading. During a healing with Joel, approximately an hour into the therapy, while I was breathing and relaxing through the pain in my spine, my surroundings changed and I forgot about the therapy I was receiving. I was standing on top of a thirty-foot flat-topped pyramid inside of a much larger pyramidal structure. Hundreds of people were assembled on all sides beneath me, and ten or so people next to me and behind me. It seemed that I was presiding over the ceremony.

I was focused on one woman in the distance, who I was perceiving as the initiate. She was walking toward the altar and ceremonially receiving the right to become a priestess. I remember holding the blue light of spiritual presence in my awareness (which I had to work to redevelop in this life) to assist the higher vibrational functions of the *Christed* self within her.

Later, I realized this woman was my present-life ex-wife and that I owed her a karmic debt even from a previous past life.

In this vision, I then felt the deceit of the people behind me, seeing them as slithering snakes. I was focused on finishing the initiation before dealing with these hostiles. As I started to feel woozy, noticing I was possibly drugged, I felt and saw an axe hit me in the back—in the same place where much of my current pain resided.

Falling forward in the vision, I tumbled down the stairs, feeling the extreme pain and sadness of not finishing my life mission. Barely alive, I was taken by the Egyptian military, directed by the priests to another location where there were three Nubian priests. My feet, hands, and penis were cut off, and my eyes had been plucked out of my face.

Hearing the incantations of the Nubians, I realized their intentions were to make sure my energy would never return to the earth. Barely conscious, holding on by the eighth chakra above my head, I was locked underground in a tomb.

Then, my consciousness was back on the table and my teacher was holding me, saying it must have been a good one. I was blown away. It took me a few days to process the vision and then a few years to work it out completely. The pain in my spine was completely released. I felt I could have done without the memories that came up for me, but they were empowering for my soul and really helped me clear much of my ego or my own personal identity separate from God.

I realize now that by telling the common people of Egypt that God was within them, I had disempowered the priesthood, which they did not like. Also, under my pacifist rule, the generals were not allowed to go to war, and they did not like that, either.

A few years later, I was reading about some pharaohs in *The Ancient Secret of the Flower of Life*, a book by Drunvalo Melchizedec. The reading matched my visions, and it helped me understand myself on a deeper level. For example, it explained why I'd had the thought when I was twelve: *If I was not going to be in charge in the world, why had I even come here?*

My guides had told me years earlier, while I was tripping on LSD, before a Grateful Dead show, that I was the last Amenhotep and that I should not walk with a strut; I should be humble. Now, I discovered from reading that this pharaoh had changed his name from Amenhotep to Akhenaton and had tried to change everyone to monotheism, or faith in one god.

Stopping the generals from going to war made them feel idle. Amon disempowered the priests by telling the people God was within them and that they did not need an intermediary. I understand why the generals and priests wanted to kill him. Now, I am so glad I do not have the kind of karma to be in charge on this planet. Really, what a mess! I'm really happy today to have a childlike incarnation, where I get to spend time playing; just the act of keeping one's mind together now, in this present life, *is enough work for anyone.*

Past lives have usually given me insights into what not to do, releasing negative personality traits and allowing me to gain awareness of a richer life—a life with a little more purpose. Past lives can build new character and provide self-knowledge into our *eternal identity.*

After I have integrated a past life, often, the people involved will show up in my present reality to be forgiven, cleansed, and interacted with as a new (or old!) friend. Interpersonal karma can be both positive and negative. As past lives emerge, you must know you are *this* now; you are not your *then*-self. A band of forgetfulness is placed on us at birth (i.e., most do not remember their past lives), but almost all of us still have the karma to work out. Once the time rift has opened for you to integrate those past lives, let those past eyes look through these eyes now, and forgive yourself and anyone else: release the karma. Remember, our goal is just to become more understanding, loving human beings by gaining mostly the realization of what not to do, by virtue of knowing what we have done in the past.

The oldest incarnation I've remembered was before I ever fell from grace: I was a blue being by the name of Vishnu. It does not matter to me if any of the incarnations were my soul, or if these higher beings just descended on me to share the stream of their energy, but it did and does feel like my own self when I have what I call a *past-life regression*.

The first memory of Vishnu came while I was sitting in the morning meditation at the Unity Church in South Lake Tahoe. Besides being a part of the hippie scene and becoming certified in body therapies, Unity Church is the only organization I ever joined. I just plain like the freedom of being allowed to walk into a church barefooted. Lots of people there like to hug. Unity is Christ-based in its foundation, and all religious or scientific beliefs are honored. One could have a Buddhist, Hindu, Islamic, or any spiritual lesson in church on any given Sunday morning. Especially fun for me is the nine-o'clock meditation that takes place before the ten-o'clock service. A half-hour of group silence in a prayerful setting really does my soul good.

During that deep silence one morning, after sitting and praying for about twenty minutes, I saw my *higher self* descend upon me from above. Then I saw myself as a blue being, with six arms and two legs. Each appendage was befitted with a spiritual tool. Just as you might see on a picture, I especially noticed the spinning discus, whirring on the index finger of one of my right hands. This was one of my few visions that did not have a negative personality flaw for me to cleanse. I felt filled with light, and my light body began to expand out from my center at least fifty feet in all directions.

Blue light filled the room and my conscious awareness. I felt extremely high for quite a while after this energetic shift. It suddenly dawned on me that the world could begin to receive this higher frequency of being. The silence and energy were like a light bath.

I understood that 1966 Germany, where I was born, had not been ready for this full-energy manifestation of the light body. In this moment of understanding, I forgave my mother for being drunk every day during my fetal process. I have always felt that I manifested attention deficit from that, and possibly other learning disabilities. She boasted that she did not smoke cigarettes or drink hard alcohol during my gestation—she drank only a six-pack of beer per day. Her motto was beer for thirst, water for washing.

In that blue light, I somehow understood God's will. I realized that my energy needed to be dampened even in her pregnancy, only to expand at the right time on earth. I've always felt since the beginning of my expansion process around 1987 that I was part of a shift of consciousness on earth—so much bigger than myself—and that my self-perceived darkness would go away as the earth plane was also awakening. I felt I would fully feel *whole* by the time the shift happened for me, for many people around the globe, and for the earth herself. The planet is a conscious entity who will also gain awareness and a celestial light body.

In that moment in that blue light, I completely forgave my mother for drinking, seeing the perfection of God's will in my life! I had already forgiven my dad for his lack of interest and participation in my life. I realized that, through his behavior, he had caused me to turn toward the light early in life, when I first began shifting. My father's neglect inadvertently helped me realize the perfection of the light and the dark working together toward the higher will.

Both my parents had enacted God's will through their free will. In fact, realizing this perfection in the universe allowed my practice of forgiveness to flourish, allowing me to trust the *divine plan* within the free will. And seeing my divine incarnation of Vishnu resolidified my trust in the divine plan for me, in this church, during meditation.

The world's unrest—all the different people who choose negative energies—and my wait for the right, loving spiritual partner, is a constant drain on my energy field. Even if I skip one day of meditation, my energy field suffers. I really needed the positive vision of my higher self at that time in Unity Church.

My next vision of this divine incarnation was not so pleasant. Joel, my Reiki master teacher, had the knack for opening peoples' past-life memories, not consciously but through his energy field. Spending time with someone who has awakened can cause awakening in your own being. He believed the Great Divine Director, one of the ascended masters who has been working with the earth and its inhabitants for hundreds of thousands of years, gave him the ability to help open others and see their past lives.

The vision of a woman's face being cut flashed through during one of my therapy sessions with Joel. It was grotesque, and I immediately pulled myself out of the vision.

A few months later, I was taking a class at Harbin Hot Springs in Lake County, California, to expand my knowledge of acupressure therapy. The teacher was a very spiritually developed and learned therapist, and Joel attended the class with me. The students would exchange sessions during class while the teacher supervised, assisted the lessons, and helped the students process as they released early childhood or past-life karma.

I perceived spiritual markings on the forehead of the woman who was about to work on me—markings only visible on the psychic plane. I told her immediately, "Get ready for a big release!" An hour passed, and nothing happened. Then my arm lifted and spontaneously dropped. The teacher came over and asked me what was going on. I told her I was feeling uncomfortable, maybe even angry. She giggled and brought me a bunch of pillows to put under my hands and feet, and she told me to just let the energy out if it came up again.

Nothing happened at first, but suddenly I felt the anger in my body and began to hit and kick the pillows. Suddenly I retrieved a memory of my dad angrily throwing and smashing a coffee cup against the wall when I was about five years old. Although I had not responded when I was little, I remembered the intensity of watching the coffee run down the wall. The intensity of that memory of my dad brought me back to the intensity of a past life, and I fully merged into that life.

***

The next two paragraphs contain explicit descriptions of a vivid vision of violence. Some readers may wish to skip this section and go to page 152.

Again I saw the woman's face being cut, but this time I saw everything around us: it was very unpleasant as I felt myself being held down in a chair by four beings who were well-dressed but looked like Cro-Magnons, with another dozen standing around and watching. The men all wore priestly garbs, and I noticed their brows were very dense, so I could tell we were in a different epoch on the earth.[3]

The punishment, it seemed, for a deified being sleeping with the temple virgin, was to watch her being cut up. I realized the head priest was also my present-life friend and teacher, Joel. The pain and guilt of the moment was so great. I managed to free myself, grabbed a sword, and impaled myself through the chest in an act of suicide. I survived for a few days, and I had some time to think about the errors of my actions.

***

[3] Hinduism suggests that our species changes, with respect to our beauty and height, depending on our proximity to the grand center of the solar system and the galactic center. The closer to the center, the more angelic we look; the further away, the more primitive.

It seems to me this was the time in history that my soul fell from *grace*, possibly many thousands of years ago. I fell from the unified field of consciousness at that time. Until the incident in this past life, of impaling myself with a sword, my soul could not truly perceive human suffering. Luckily, God gave me this gift to understand myself more deeply, allowing my soul to grow.

Since we are all eternal beings, we live in order to infuse personality into our eternity. On this plane, we get to choose to remember our soul's perfection, within free will.

As Swami Subramunia said, "The outer reality seems real."

Many blessings came from that past life vision. As I began to release the guilt from my soul and my physical body, yet another physical pain in my back had been released, and more karma began to unwind itself.

According to Hinduism, the solar cycle lasts approximately 25,000 years, the galactic cycle about 250,000 thousand years, and the universal cycle lasts about 2,500,000 years. The dark points return halfway through the solar cycle, and while we are farthest away, we lose consciousness of our unity with God. It is interesting that Jesus came to Earth during this darker period of the solar cycle. My guru, Swami Sri Yukteswar, noted that we are out of the Kali Yuga ("age of Kali", or the age of darkness) now, and the galactic cycle is also on its way back to the light.

SHAPESHIFTING

AS WE SURRENDER TO THE *universal mind*, more and more, we become all that we are, which is comprised of all physical life, all the angelic realms, and all the dimensions within and outside of this plane of existence. In this state of surrender, our visual and auditory range becomes enhanced. Part of this journey involves incorporating the part of us that exists in all the animal kingdoms.

It is vital to understand that when any life form on earth goes extinct, we are hurting part of our multidimensional selves.

The first shift I experienced occurred early on at one of the Grateful Dead shows I attended in Angels Camp, California, just after I had turned twenty-one. The energies at the show were already very high. With my attention deeply focused on the music and with a very focused deep breathing practice I'd developed after a couple years of doing yoga, I suddenly felt taller, perhaps nine or ten feet tall, and I saw myself from behind my head. I felt like a giant *cobra*. Specifically, I noticed the cobra hood as it expanded very wide, opening my vision to encompass all the people around me.

It was such a trip to see how things looked from the perspective of another dimension. The high energies of the upper chakras coursing through my body felt wonderful. As I looked upward, I intuitively recognized what I thought of at the time as the "government mind." I felt like this mind-like fence was trying to hold people down to a lower plane of consciousness. Without hesitating, I pushed through and past the "government mind" into the outer atmosphere, knowing nothing could stop my *God consciousness.* The darkness had no hold on me. The entire experience only lasted a few minutes, and then I was back to my normal state of awareness—but full of joy, and I still felt taller.

Another such animal shift came at age twenty-three, while I was with a girlfriend. The relationship lasted less than two months, but it was intense. We had met in Tahoe through a mutual friend and felt immediately attracted to each other. As we spoke, we found ourselves quite compatible.

The playful and sexual energy between us was phenomenal. We were lying together and rolling around when we both had the feeling of being *lions.* I had a quick vision of being in another place, where I was surrounded by several other lions. She and I agreed we had both remembered the same past lifetime as lions. Nothing else happened, but it struck me how playful lions are.

Minutes after having the vision of the lions, I went into another room. Suddenly, the entire room was filled with golden electric light, and the feeling of an angelic presence surrounded me. A telepathic communication told me that it was Archangel Michael, whose presence told me I was now courting his twin flame. As I felt slightly embarrassed, he assured me they did not have monogamous jealousy in the higher planes and I was not in any kind of trouble. He just wanted me to relay a message to her that he was her spiritual partner and that he had been trying to contact her.

When I rejoined her, I felt a little awkward telling her about the communication I had received. To my surprise, she was incredibly receptive to the idea. In fact, she had very deep feelings on the subject; she told me she had received a written letter in the mail from Michael the previous year, which had confused her greatly. It turned out the communication I had just had was the confirmation she had been waiting for.

I was so glad I shared the information and was not too embarrassed to tell her my experience. Other times, I have felt moved to say something to someone but have held back, fearing their response. With most people, sharing my inner truth has gone over well. But not everyone is ready to hear God expressing through someone, so they only see me as the individual and receive the message with their ego instead of their soul's deep awareness.

I have had several other shapeshifts over the years, but I will share only one more here: some years later when I was in my early thirties, one of my most significant shifts happened at the Rainbow Gathering in Montana on National Forest land. As I entered the gathering site, my awareness was immediately drawn to a lay line, one of the earth's energetic meridian lines. The line ran through the middle of the gathering, and I stepped over it as I was looking for a spot to camp. I did not want to touch it because it was completely black, and I did not feel compelled to do any energetic clearing work on it at the time.

A couple days later, it was time for the six-hour silent meditation for world peace, which is the purpose of the Rainbow Family gatherings each year. During the middle of the sixth hour of meditation, I shifted. During most of the meditation, I had been praying in a deep indigo light. I was disturbed, though, by people whispering behind me and by a dog in the circle that was intermittently growling.

Feeling how important this silence was to achieve world peace, I became increasingly agitated by this disruptive noise, and I suddenly found myself making a strong, silent command into the universe: "I AM the only voice here." Before this moment, I had not thought of myself as having that kind of authority over my own reality. I felt as if I could rule the silence. I am not sure if the command worked for anyone else, but it sure worked for me. I was quiet.

My consciousness jetted backward immediately, and from my spiritual body, I could see I had taken the shape of a 20-foot-long dragon its body an earthy, deep green. As soon as I saw the dragon, I felt myself move forward and merge into it. I could feel the wings holding me down, connecting to the earth. It was probably the most grounded I have ever felt. This solid and grounded feeling merged with the dragon's mind, setting us free in the universe to fly without thought or hindrances. It was a breathtaking experience. I was grounded and flying at the same time.

My next thought was of the black earth lay line I had crossed on my way into the gathering a couple days prior. My notion was that the dragon's energy probably had a deeper connection to the Mother Earth, and so, I began to look at the line and pray for the earth. I spent the rest of the time focusing on the meridian to bring light into it, and I prayed for the earth's *ascension*. The light finally merged into the black, and I watched it all turn to gold.

All of earth's meridians will have to turn to light. Just like us as people, I believe the Mother Earth is also in an ascension process. When Mother Earth makes her shift into the higher planes, all the people who have tried to ascend in past incarnations but found it difficult will be able to make the shift. Do not give up!

As I opened my eyes, everything had returned to normal. The meditation had just ended, and people around me were intoning the spiritual sound, *aum ("om")*. As I had much energy flowing for the next several hours, I began to do energy work on the people around me who wanted it.

Only a month later, while sitting in the Lake Tahoe casino health club where I was working, I felt a density as I tried to go into meditation, and I became frustrated. Internally, I heard the voice of one of my guides very audibly saying, "Just move your dragon's neck."

Without thinking, I moved my head and felt the very long neck. Previously, I had felt the body, wings, and mind. This time, I felt the muscle texture and connective tissues and fluids in my neck. I admit, it was a little weird, but it was a fascinating experience. The big dragon energy easily pushed away the density of the casino. The altered state came so easily, and I went into a deep meditation. The energy of the dragon lasted only a few minutes, but the focus on God continued for the rest of the day.

Almost every shift or experience I have ever had has occurred only once. I believe that once we have experienced another dimension, it integrates into us permanently. I have also experienced integration with whales, spiders, lobsters, and many other living things. It is always just an energetic shift; my body does not actually change on the physical plane.

Spider energy is the culmination of all our fears, and it is a huge and terrorizing shift to experience and then release. It is very important, though, to integrate to access the eight-appendage energy of the Hindu deities. We may have to go through many cosmic shifts seemingly on our own, but believe me, there are always guides present to help you through those big ones.

RENUNCIATIONS

THERE ARE MANY NEGATIVE OR harmful things I have been able to release from my life, and there are many things I still hold on to. I live by the assumption that when some negative trait or desire is ready to leave me, it will surface for me to work on so that only those things closer to the wholeness that is my true desire will remain. Certain desires have just fallen away as I have embodied more truth.

We do not need to make a concerted effort to stop doing something negative—for example, overeating or smoking. You already know it is not great for you, but when you enter your true wholeness, these negative habits will surface and naturally fall away.

When we are ready, we can also create the opportunity to release negative karma by fasting—for one day, or three days, or even a month. Alternatively, we can choose to not speak for an amount of time. We can choose to abstain from electronic media, opting to sit in periods of meditation. We can choose to not go shopping or drinking, or it could be just letting go of negative thought patterns for a determined period.[4]

Renunciations of any kind will create fruition in your mind. In other words, any time we give something up, we create space for something new to enter.

If you become aware of a dependency or a negative tendency, allow it to dissolve. As we set the goal of attaining enlightenment, it becomes easier to release the things that are not in line with that goal. One might not even have to think of letting go or cultivating a spiritual practice as an austerity—but for a loving and conscious person, things fall away at the right time.

It is not helpful to punish yourself for consuming that next cigarette or steak fillet; at the right time, the habit will fall away. When you do make the decision for a cleaner life, spirit recognizes your efforts and rewards you by assisting your efforts. And really, you are rewarding yourself. When we are working toward an eternal state of awareness, the universe always recognizes our efforts. Simultaneously, spirit and the universe support all of our decisions.

The more we renounce unhealthy mental patterns, activities, or anything else, doors open for more healthy fun.

In my own life, I have noticed replacing negative habits with positive ones really works. Adding yoga to your life is great, but be sure to add playtime too—whatever you enjoy. For me, I never thought it would happen, but I also really enjoy going to church. If

---

[4] The tradition of committing to periods of abstinence is found across many cultures and religions, including Ramadan (Islam) and Lent (Christianity), to name a few.

it is open-minded, any church or spiritual practice is fun for me. Of course, a good festival is the same for me, because when I'm dancing or hanging out with people coming together and having fun, I feel at my best.

Chronic pessimism is one example of a negative attachment. There are always many positive things going on. If we cannot prevent the negativities we perceive, we might as well not get stuck on them.

As previously mentioned, a steady yoga practice is the most beneficial habit I can suggest to replace the things you do not want in your life. Directing your attention to the conscious union with the divine is always the fastest method to attaining yogic goals. In fact, the purpose of yoga is to achieve the state of union with God. By staying in the moment, breathing and relaxing, and moving in the light that you are, you will eventually know God.

In India, some yogis have no possessions. They do not stay in any one location very long, they are rarely sexually motivated, and they rarely have money or even comb their hair. Eastern cultures tend to support this lifestyle. However, dropping out of society is not great for a Western yogi, because Western society does not support a true spiritual intention or way of life. For me, becoming dependent on spirit no longer means letting go of society. *Living in spirit* is living with trust—knowing I can deal with whatever comes, either internally or what is presented externally.

This type of total detachment is practiced in the hope of meeting God. Most yogis I have met who practice for long periods in their life agree on this point. Of course, in my mind, being unattached becomes another attachment in and of itself. Therefore, striving for total non-attachment, I follow my natural desires, which I believe are God-given.

Already knowing God, I am just being my natural self. If I want something, I have it. It is good to have desire, enjoy it. If I am happy, it is so; and if I am angry, I allow that as well, albeit briefly.

How we express ourselves is important. You can feel anger without being violent toward another person. If we are truly feeling, we will stay in the truth. Negative feelings are not caused by a past experience; it is this moment that matters. The heart is in this moment always connecting to the mind.

I have heard of His Holiness the Dalai Lama putting people on retreat for more than twenty years. These monks live alone and eat a few grains of rice per day. Left to go into deep meditative states, these monks are able to resolve many of their past-life karmas. They suggest that what is important is *this life* and working toward the next life. Personally, I believe what the Course in Miracles suggests: growth happens in relationships, and the more difficult the relationship, the higher the potential for growth. If we are in a cave, we have a relationship with ourselves and God. I find it is relationships with other people that can really cause us to reflect strongly on ourselves.

SRI AMMA

IN THE EARLY 1990S, I hitchhiked from California to New Hampshire for the international Rainbow Gathering, where I reconnected with one of my favorite people, Sanan. He is who I would consider a renegade Krishna devotee, like myself—staying devoted without a formal, organized practice. He told me he was driving back to California and that I could hitch a ride, but first, he was going to New York to meet with the Holy Mother from India: Amritanandamayi, better known as Amma, or Ammachi ("Mother"). I gave him my last thirty dollars for gas money, and off we went to New York. I thought it would be fun to meet a Hindu holy person; I had already met the Holy Spirit and the masters. Even though I have always felt like a child and not a master, I felt holy by then, aware of God in myself and in my interactions.

I thought to myself, *Holy Mother Schmoly Mother.* Why was someone holier than anyone else? As I entered the line of a hundred people waiting for a hug from her. She was known as the "hugging saint." It's funny: hugging people was already a spiritual practice of mine. During that time of my life, I loved taking people into the higher planes during a long hug. People had to be willing to let go of their body, but not everyone could let go in that way, and I didn't force anyone. Of course, there is still nothing better than a real, deep hug.

As I neared the front of the line, I began to perceive her supernatural activity. Basically, I saw her pulling stuck energies out of people's chakras. When I got a few feet away, with just a couple of people in front of me, I heard her say to me psychically, "Let me see your pee-pee." As I looked down, my whole perception changed: I regressed into a child of about five years old. I was naked and could see my penis. My skin color was deep indigo. In that moment, I realized she was spiritually my *mother* and could perceive every thought that I had. I was completely humbled!

I was next in line to receive the hug. I tried to look at her, but instead, I felt my eyes being forced upward. I was still a few feet away when I saw the white light over her head. My eyes were pushed upward by an invisible force, and I saw the same light above my own head. Our lights merged. In my next conscious moment, we were in a deep embrace, cheeks touching.

The swami next to us was pulling on my arm, freaking out because I had done more than just put my head in her lap, as is traditionally appropriate. Even at the swami level, he did not see our spiritual interaction. Amma turned to him and said, "Leave him alone; this is my son." Then the swami allowed me to hug her for a while in a beautiful moment of peace. I walked away in peace and sat back into meditation in the crowd.

Later during this visit, a group of Amma's devotees invited me to lunch. It turned out they really wanted to know why Amma was *smiling* during our hug. They told me she was always feeling people's grief, and she usually would reflect the sadness others felt. I did not know why, which I told them.

I have enjoyed seeing Amma every few years when she tours the United States. The peace she brings is phenomenal. Her events are always free, but of course, people can donate to her causes. She directs orphanages in India, and she is a very giving person on an international level, creating homes and bringing food and water to people in need. In my experience, she is one of the few actual living masters on earth.

SWAMI SATHYA SAI BABA

MY FIRST INTERACTION WITH SWAMI Sai Baba occurred just a few months after meeting Amma. At that time, around age twenty-four, I was ostensibly dropped out of society, living out of my tent on the island of Kauai.

I was attending a weekly drum circle gathering. At these gatherings, everyone was welcome, and almost everyone was very laid back. Pot smoking was prevalent, while alcohol was mainly absent. Many of the attendees were in prayer while drumming. Nobody wore a tie! The drum circle had about forty people in attendance, and everything was going well. Suddenly, I remembered some sacred ashes in my possession I had been given a few months earlier by Baba Kali, a wandering monk I had met in Tahoe. He'd told me the ashes were made by a Hindu holy man named Sai Baba. The thought came to me to finally use the ashes and smudge everyone's forehead in the circle.

Putting my drum down and moving around in a circle, I began to apply the ashes to people's foreheads. With each person I smudged, I also did a quick blessing prayer. Everyone accepted the blessing—except for one person. When I approached him, he said, "I do not want this." I told him the ashes were from a Hindu Holy man. He responded, "I *am* a Hawaiian holy man." I continued around the circle, and everyone else received the ashes. I got back to my spot, but for some reason, I was bothered to the point where I could not even drum. I felt the Hawaiian holy man was in my space, maybe not on purpose, but I just could not pull any kind of beat together. I went into deep prayer and asked God what to do. To my surprise, the answer to my prayer came from Sai Baba directly. He flew toward me as everything else vanished, and with a large smile, said, "Do this!" A flood of golden love light came from his forehead toward the Hawaiian man. Immediately, his energy stopped interfering with me psychically and melted into a sense of deep peace. I could again play the drum, and the drum circle took off. Joy filled the circle—no more negative thoughts for a long time. After the vision, I realized I could have done that on my own, but I had not had the presence of mind to take the action.

About three years later, after reintegrating somewhat into society, I was working as a massage therapist at a hotel back home in South Lake Tahoe. I remembered the money I'd saved and that I had promised myself to go to India when I had enough saved. I went to my supervisor at the hotel and casino and told them I was quitting to spend two months in India. Graciously, the supervisor told me my job would be waiting for me upon my return. I think if I had asked for the time off, they probably would have said no! The universe supports us when we really make up our mind about what we want to do.

INDIA

I ASKED MY GIRLFRIEND OF the time, who later became my wife, to go there with me, but she was afraid. So, I booked a round-trip ticket with a return in two months and set off alone.

I landed in New Delhi at 2:00 a.m. in the beginning of October of 1993. A taxicab took me to a random hotel. At 4:00 a.m., I was still lying awake, restless. Although I had stopped watching television regularly, I turned on the one in the hotel room. To my major disappointment, MTV was on. Tears streamed down my cheeks. I had thought I was getting away from the Western world. I turned off the TV and finally slept a for a couple of hours.

I found the Indian people to be organized and effective at making money off tourists, so for the first couple of days, I paid too much for everything. My first couple of days in India were arduous. The extreme wealth alongside poverty was shocking. People lived in tiny shacks next to high-rise buildings. Occasionally, on a long walk, I would have to step over a dead body, but the locals assured me it would be picked up within days. Within the first few days of my trip,

I felt I could not stay in this place for two months, and again, tears rolled down my cheek.

People were defecating and urinating in the streets. I could not understand why until I went into a public urinal. The stench was so bad, I could not decide whether to pee or throw up!

In the next days, I found myself being hustled by various tourist agencies and taxis. I finally found an all-day sightseeing trip in a private taxi that cost me about twenty dollars. We visited many sights and temples, which I enjoyed. Finally, the next day, I found the official government of India travel agency, a legitimate organization promoting national tourism; they were not in on the hustle that seem to be happening everywhere else. I procured an Indian Railways unlimited rail ticket for three hundred US dollars. Now, for one month, I could travel anywhere, anytime, throughout India.

By the third day, everything had come together, albeit slowly. While sitting in a park, I met an Indian Sikh. His home was in Canada, but he was back in India to visit his family. He spoke perfect English and helped me without expecting any personal gain.

We went to a Sikh temple, which I thought was great, because I've always loved seeing how different people worship. He then helped me understand the difficult train systems and taught me how to find my way. He was absolutely a godsend. The next best thing was the *Lonely Planet* guidebook, as it really helped me find my way around.

Before landing in India, I stopped in Germany to visit my grandmother and sister. It was great to be with my family in Bonn, the town where I was born. I had not seen them for a long time, and it felt good to speak German again.

Every city I have ever visited has its own energetic culture that is more or less conductive to spiritual energies. For years living in Tahoe and Hawaii, I had become used to delving into a deep blue and gold light and merging with God during my meditation practices. In addition, I had never had any problems sleeping. However, the culture in Bonn was so energetically dense that I was sleeping terribly, and my meditations led to headaches from trying to push light through the electromagnetic (mental-emotional) fields there. The combination World-War history; the gothic churches; and the incredibly dense diet consisting of meat, potatoes, and beer was not conducive to spiritual energies.

By contrast, in India, surrounded by the spiritual, vegetarian culture, I had some of the best meditations of my life, bathing in golden light with my eyes wide open. In India, I experienced bliss—even while sitting in rail stations in what would normally be the boredom of waiting for a train. In India, it was so much easier to keep my thoughts on God than it had been in Germany. It was good to experience the difference between the cultural energies. It taught me much about energetic densities in different locations.

My second day just wandering around New Delhi, I stumbled upon a Siva temple. There was a pleasant man outside sitting next to the entrance, and with a hand gesture, he invited me to come in. I took off my shoes and entered the compound. The temple room was small, maybe fifteen feet by fifteen feet, with a beautiful four-foot square altar in the center and a large bell hanging in the middle of the room. There was nobody inside, so I sat in a corner and began to meditate.

After a small amount of time, one man came in and poured milk over the deity statues. Witnessing the loving devotional acts from the devotees was incredible. I was having a bit of trouble quieting my mind, but about half an hour later, I noticed a young Hindu woman in the other corner reading scripture in devotional practice. I hadn't noticed her joining me, and I didn't notice when she left.

While she was reading in Hindi, I saw a light over her head, and immediately I began to hear words in German. The spirit was using her sound vibrations to communicate with me. I don't believe I was actually hearing what she was reading; however, the voice was guiding my meditation, telling me where to look and how to breathe and clearing energies in my own field.

As my chakra system came into alignment, I felt my energy line up. My vision opened behind my head, and I saw my light body change into a serpent as my energy got higher. Then the serpent locked position facing upward, changing into what seemed like a rod of iron—another immobilizing state of energy beyond the serpent in the upper chakras. Any comprehensible perception of myself was dissolved for an inestimable amount of time after that. I was in absolute silence. Sometime later, I felt myself descending and settled back into my body. I knew the experience was done.

When I went back outside the temple, the man was still there, smiling. As our gazes merged, we fell into a deep bliss. He motioned with his hand upward, we disconnected, and I felt and saw white light pouring down my third eye and all around me. I sat down fifty feet away, and about twenty little children came and played around me for about an hour.

This was the first of many big visual and auditory conscious shifts that were granted to my being while I was visiting India. During that month, I visited every type of church, mosque, temple, and spiritual organization available, and I always felt some type of interaction with God's spirit.

The biggest shifts for me happened while I was staying at the Sathya Sai Baba ashram, Prasanthi Nilayam: The Abode of the Highest Peace. This is Swami Sai Baba's main ashram, near Sai Baba's birthplace, in Puttaparthy, Andra Pradesh, near Bangalore. He was born into total poverty.

When I first saw Swami, I had just walked into the compound, and I caught a peek through a crack in the fence. The sight of him overwhelmed me. His countenance was so strong that I dropped my head in humility, just like when I first stepped into the huge temple compound. I bowed to God as I stepped under the aum symbol on the front gate. There was a strong visible charge of electric white light throughout the temple, a light I could feel and see, and for the first time since being in India, I felt safety and peace permeating my being.

I decided to stay there, and I immediately booked a spot in the onsite dorms for six days—and I ended up staying for twenty-four days in total. Swami said that people who traveled far to see him deserved a safe place to stay. It was about five dollars a night to stay. Hindus from nearby had to book hotel rooms outside of the compound unless they had special permission from Swami.

The compound was probably a square mile, with rooms for couples as well as dorms for one. I bought a mattress and scored a mosquito net left behind by someone else. If you are going to India, here is a tip: bring a mosquito net. There were about thirty people per dorm, and there was a feeling of unity with the others, who were also there on spiritual pilgrimage. There seemed to be devotees from every country in the world, and some nationalities split into their own groups for spiritual singing on their own time. However, everyone came together in the morning and in the evening for prayer and song.

Though I had not planned it, I arrived at the ashram in November just before Swami's seventieth birthday. My first week there was very quiet, as only a few thousand people were at the ashram, so it was easy to move around and make it to meditations as well as morning and night worship. Then as his birthday drew near, more than a hundred thousand people came for the celebration. He hosted everyone with lots of music and food in the temple, although most Hindus had to get an outside hotel.

Sometimes, Baba would come out in the mornings, and sometimes, he would not show himself. When he did come out, it was considered a blessing, or *darshan* (the beholding of a deity). I attended the daily events, but once the large birthday crowds showed up, I retreated to the hills and meditated on the rocks above the ashram.

Because Baba had many spiritual powers and abilities, it seemed everyone wanted something from him: a private interview, healing, wealth, marriage for their daughters, and so on. He told people, "Do not ask me for an interview, but instead ask me for *inner-view*." Swami said it was in God's nature to give, and the closer you were to spirit, the more it would be in your nature to give, in contrast to asking for too much.

One could tell when he was pleased or excited because he would throw thousands of candies into the crowd. They seemed to appear out of thin air as he waved his arms. He gave people cheap trinkets with his picture on them, and sometimes, he would give away an expensive Rolex watch to one of his devotees, in private.

He also created mounds of ashes that he produced from a small vase. I observed him do this. The ash was packaged and given away, to be used for healing, prayers, meditative connections, and adornments on people's altars. He claimed ashes were as close as the physical plane could get to the spiritual plane. Swami could also teleport an object from one location to another, manifest multiple bodies, be in more than one location at a time, and communicate telepathically, all of which I was privileged to personally witness.

Many people want to discredit Swami as a trickster, but I witnessed his spiritual power many times, and was personally only ever blessed by him.

***

The first day at the ashram, after finding a place to sleep and settling in to where I was, I took a nice walk around the compound. During my walk, I thought to myself, *I wonder if I will meet a nice girl here.*

Psychically— although it sounded as if it were right in my face— someone yelled, "What?" I realized that not only was I *not* there for that, but I sincerely was *not* alone in my mind with Swami present. I paid much more attention to my thoughts after that moment of being psychically busted. The rest of the time in the ashram was similar, and even though I had practiced watching my thoughts before, the intensity of my awareness in every moment grew at the ashram as I felt governed by Swami.

The second morning I sat with a few thousand people along with Swami in meditation, and I was overwhelmed with bliss. Sitting there, it felt as if something were being pulled out of my forehead, like a fishing line, which I could see after a while. It looked like a string of white light a few feet from my forehead, continuously being pulled out, curling, and disappearing into nothing.

It was a bizarre thing to feel and see. In fact, this meditation with thousands of others was nearly overwhelming. However, after an hour or so, I relaxed into it. The white light string experience lasted five or six hours, part of which I spent partly sitting in meditation and partly walking around the compound. Nobody looked at me, as if I were invisible, and I could walk anywhere on the compound, which was usually restricted to the masses. Still, I mostly sat as the experience continued. It seemed as if my karma was being pulled out slowly, or I suppose it could have been quickly; either way, it was intense but uniquely blissful.

As the days continued, every day with Baba was another cool spiritual experience. The intensity did not stop the entire time I was at the ashram. Sometimes I would find myself suddenly out of body; other times, Swami would deliver a lecture to the crowd and inspire the most amazing insights.

One night during a lucid dream, I flew with Swami at incredible speed to somewhere in Africa. There, he showed me many different percussive rhythms on old logs, programming them into my body consciousness rather than my mind. Sometimes, the various rhythmic structures I learned come out in the present day, while I am drumming.

Every morning and evening, meditations and singing ensued in worship of the *supreme*. On the sixth day I was there, while sitting with Swami, I became aware of how much work it would be to hold spiritual consciousness in the world, and I was reduced to tears. As the days progressed, I found myself in tears while in his presence several times as I perceived the gravity of the work to be done on earth and on myself, alongside beautiful perfection of everything.

***

Baba had to trick me to get me to merge into the light on my own.

The big crowds there for Swami's seventieth birthday had left before my last couple of days at the ashram, but on this morning toward the end of my stay, there were still more than ten thousand people sitting in the mass meditation. Sai Baba believed that when people slept at night, they lost their higher state of awareness. Because of this, he told people to "wake God up every morning."

We are all potentially at the center of the universe, when our mental radio is dialed in to the God station. During this meditation, I was brought into a mental debate with the crowd, which lasted about an hour. I heard psychic voices telling me not to say that I was at one with God because "Swami's a jealous God." It seemed reasonable to me that if Swami were at one with God, he would also want that for me and for everyone else.

Simultaneously, I was working on my mind; I really wanted to accept the presence of the divine everywhere and in myself, and I wanted to own my wholeness.

I did not want to get sucked into idol worship. The awareness of the mistake I had made during a past incarnation made me want to avoid repeating that kind of spiritual mistake. My perspective on making mistakes has now shifted; I still make perfect *spirit*-guided mistakes constantly, which help me grow.

The voices continued, "Worship Swami. He's a jealous God!" Although I accepted that God was in Swami and would have listened to whatever he told me, I could not fully agree that jealousy should be part of God. In the core of my being, I knew that if Swami were God, he also wanted me to be one with God, and he did not wish to usurp power. The psychic voices of the *one mind* in the crowd continued. Finally, I'd had enough! I felt a little angry at the internal debate, and I am not sure if I yelled it out loud or simply thought it loudly, but I commanded one word: *Silence*! It is funny that in all my previous years of bliss, from when I first realized God until I merged into the white light, I did not get myself into that uppermost chakra, but finally, with the sincerity and truth of *anger*, I merged into the *Ocean of Milk* (pure white light) into the sixth chakra (the third-eye chakra), above me and out of my body.[5]

---

[5] Hinduism suggests that Vishnu sits in the Ocean of Milk, and it was at that moment I realized I had come to the next part of my spiritual name: *Vishnu*.

I existed effortlessly, with no direction, no time, no thought. I think this white-light meditation experience lasted about an hour, until I felt my conscious awareness settle back in and descend into my body. I was motionless for another hour after that and felt the light pouring down on me from above while I sat still, immobilized.

Still frozen in place, if I felt a thought from outside myself: all I had to do was move a finger to stop it. My constant inner debate about idol worship was over. The years of working on myself had brought me into a deep peace at the recognition of the absolute presence and power with which we are all one and from which we only become separated from by our mind's activities.

By the end of my three-and-a-half-week stay with Swami, I had realized that with God, all things are possible. I found what I sought when I finally merged into the white light and found a deep, perfect peace! I learned that the absolute presence of God was not separate from myself: we are the expression of God.

***

The first time I merged into the *white light* when I was just nineteen, I could just see it everywhere like rows of diamonds. That event started my search for truth. Even though it happened because I had hurt my knee, it had been a gift from the Holy Spirit. The second time I saw the light, I was still aware of my body, and it was a gift of the Holy Mother, Amma, sharing her own connection with God. Now, after the third time with Swami, I knew the first two times had been gifts.

We all have many teachers throughout our many lives and incarnations. Some of our teachers are positive and some are negative; some will give and some will try to absorb your power. Remember that the true power is really the *power of love*. Always trust the universe in yourself and all around you. After all, we are all waking up from a cosmic dream: the dream of individual life. We can choose to see the divine plan and trust the ultimate outcome. God truly is alive in all things, and His is a long plan.

Everyone has the right to know our *mother-father* God in ourselves, which is ultimately our heavenly birthright. At the higher stages of God consciousness, the positive and the negative work together for the greater good. Each person on earth is at a different place spiritually with respect to what they must learn. The third dimension needs much help, as we are now in a new galactic day and people will more easily see the darkness in our corporations, governments, Big Pharma, banking institutions, and themselves.

My deepest feeling is that at my point of merging into the white light, all the masters decided I needed more earth time to evolve. On some level, I thought I would not come back from merging into the white light. But obviously, there was more for me to do: from washing dishes to continuing to clear some negative beliefs to helping people along their own spiritual paths.

It turned out all I needed to learn was be human, participate in life, and learn how to play. I was shown after my white-light experience that I had done enough work in other lifetimes and this time I should work more on being a kid.

The day after my mergence, I was surprised to find myself looking at baby clothes. I thought the clothes would be a nice present for my girlfriend back in Lake Tahoe. I had not thought about having a child since high school, and for a few years, I had believed I would become a monk. Now, with true self-knowledge acquired through meditation, I knew that monastic life was not my soul's path. To my further surprise, my girlfriend became pregnant about a week after I got back from India. I bought her a ring in India, and I proposed to her the day after I returned to the States.

About ten months after I returned from India, my son, Isaac (with the initials: I.A.M.), was born. We had a home birth. At the moment of his birthing, a dense golden light filled the room with love. After the birthing process, I took him to the altar and sat in meditation with him for at least an hour, the gold light still permeating my vision. Holding him as a baby, I had some of the best meditations ever, making sure he had stable psychic peace.

As I perceived his most recent past incarnation, I was privileged to see some of the karma I could help him to overcome. I was told by my guides that he had come from the heavenly city of Shambhala and had been waiting for a parent to merge into the white light; his soul needed to be brought up in truth and never lied to. I am glad to say I never lied to him, and I allowed him to see my shortcomings by not pretending to know something I didn't.

During Isaac's birthing process, Swami appeared in the room, above the altar I had built in our bedroom. Just before Isaac began to crown, I turned to see Swami Sai Baba looking at us with a big loving smile. I looked back at the crowning baby, and I noticed the sun was rising. I looked back at Swami, who was just smiling wordlessly. Then the baby pushed out. The nurse-midwife gave me the scissors, and I cut the cord and placed the newborn on my wife's chest. As the room was filled with golden light, I was overcoming deep bliss to be able to act at all. I forgot all about Swami's presence as the baby completely captured my attention.

Beginning when I was nineteen and over the years during times of learning or need, I have seen ascended masters, including Swami Sai Baba; my original guru, Yogananda; the Lord Christ; Lord Krishna; Saint Germaine; Mother Mary; Amma; and Quan Yin (Guanyin), the Chinese goddess of mercy. These light beings seem to be the core of my soul group. I have also seen more rarely many of the great hosts of angels or other light beings who are indescribable. I mostly see them while needing to hold myself or some part of reality together and during other crucial periods of extreme planetary psychic need. Sometimes I have seen them in the form of a full *light body*; other times, their faces might just flow by so I know they are present. Alternatively, I might just hear their voice during these moments, and any fear or worry leaves me immediately.

All I know is that the saints, masters, and angels cannot help us until we are ready to let go of our own fear and suffering. This is the true meaning of free will. Karmic law simply states that as human beings, what we allow will be allowed and what we do not allow will not be allowed. We must recognize for ourselves the truth of the power of love. Who really knows what is best for someone else's evolution besides themselves? Everyone perceives God a little differently.

God needs our love just as much as we need to be loved. The presence in us gets stronger, works through us, and becomes more loving as we evolve spiritually.

Swami's motto was "Love all. Serve all."

I am sure the ascended masters had shortcomings before they became perfected, as we all do. It is through our shortcomings that we truly learn and God learns through our own learning on earth.

God gave every culture its own religiosity; each culture holds a piece of the puzzle toward our collective evolution. The Mother Earth is a conscious being who is awakening at this activation time. It will become easier to shift or harder, depending on the side you choose. All choices will be honored, and people choosing a third-dimensional planet with war and struggle will be allowed that option. But I certainly see a split in awareness, and both sides are getting more intense—the light becoming lighter and the dark becoming more evident.

***

I remember driving down the road around the age of thirty-six, in a state of frustration because I had not been able to talk to Jesus for over a year. I begged him to speak with me. I told him I felt very uncomfortable. He finally spoke and said, "Arjang, you *are* comfort!" I could have disagreed, but I know he was right. I relaxed into my heart chakra and felt the peace of my being. Then he asked me, "What is spiritual maturity?" After a minute, I told him I did not know.

Then Jesus said to me, "An *Open Door.*"

I knew he did not just mean to open the door of my house to people. He meant I needed to open the door of my heart to everyone.

APPENDIX: SUGGESTED FURTHER READING

The Holy Science by Swami Sri Yukteswar Giri (originally written under the title "Kaivalya Darsanam")

Nine Faces of Christ, by Eugene E. Whitworth

The Fire from Within, by Carlos Castaneda

Life and Teaching of the Masters of the Far East, by Baird Spalding (book series)

The Further Education of Oversoul Seven, by Jane Roberts (second book of the *Oversoul Seven* trilogy)

Watch Your Dreams, by Ann Ree Colton

Other Works Mentioned:

A Course in Miracles, by Helen Schucman

Lonely Planet India, (Country Guide) by Lonely Planet